WINNING IN FOREIGN MARKETS
Your Global Guide®

Michele Forzley

A FIFTY-MINUTE™ SERIES BOOK

CRISP PUBLICATIONS, INC.
Menlo Park, California

WINNING IN FOREIGN MARKETS
Your Global Guide®

Michele Forzley

Global Guide is a registered trademark of Michele Forzley.

CREDITS
Managing Editor: **Kathleen Barcos**
Editor: **Follin Armfield**
Typesetting: **ExecuStaff**
Cover Design: **Carol Harris / David Barcos**
Artwork: **Ralph Mapson**

Copyright © 1994 by Crisp Publications, Inc.

Printed in the United States of America by Bawden Printing Company.

English language Crisp books are distributed worldwide. Our major international distributors include:

CANADA: Reid Publishing Ltd., Box 69559—109 Thomas St., Oakville, Ontario, Canada L6J 7R4. TEL: (905) 842-4428, FAX: (905) 842-9327

Raincoast Books Distribution Ltd., 112 East 3rd Avenue, Vancouver, British Columbia, Canada V5T 1C8. TEL: (604) 873-6581, FAX: (604) 874-2711

AUSTRALIA: Career Builders, P.O. Box 1051, Springwood, Brisbane, Queensland, Australia 4127. TEL: 841-1061, FAX: 841-1580

NEW ZEALAND: Career Builders, P.O. Box 571, Manurewa, Auckland, New Zealand. TEL: 266-5276, FAX: 266-4152

JAPAN: Phoenix Associates Co., Mizuho Bldg. 2-12-2, Kami Osaki, Shinagawa-Ku, Tokyo 141, Japan. TEL: 3-443-7231, FAX: 3-443-7640

Selected Crisp titles are also available in other languages. Contact International Rights Manager Suzanne Kelly at (415) 323-6100 for more information.

Library of Congress Catalog Card Number 93-73144
Forzley, Michele
Winning in Foreign Markets
ISBN 1-56052-254-2

This book is printed on recyclable paper with soy ink.

ABOUT THIS BOOK

Winning in Foreign Markets is not like most books. It stands out in an important way. It is not a book to read—it is a book to *use*. The "self-paced" format and many worksheets encourage readers to get involved and try new ideas immediately.

International trade and marketing is rapidly becoming the business trend. This book will help you capitalize on this trend by providing information on how to find resources, learn international trade terminology and develop a market-entry strategy to expand your business and your bottom line.

Winning in Foreign Markets can be used effectively a number of ways. Here are some possibilities:

- **Individual Study.** Because the book is self-instructional, all that you need is a quiet place, committed time, and a pencil. By completing the activities and exercises, you receive both valuable feedback and action steps to understanding international business and finding markets worldwide.

- **Workshops and Seminars.** This book was developed from hundreds of interactive seminars and contains many exercises that work well with group participation. The book is also a refresher for future reference by workshop attendees.

- **Remote Location Training.** This book is an excellent self-study resource for managers, supervisors, and managerial candidates not able to attend home office training sessions.

Even after this book has been used for training and applied to real situations, it will remain a valuable source of ideas for reflection.

PREFACE

In today's world, understanding and joining the global marketplace is fundamental to a business's success.

All businesses, often at their founding, devoted effort to understanding the markets for the products or services the company offered. This knowledge led to decisions being made on what to sell and to whom, and on how to sell, package, price and promote. It directed how resources were allocated.

Most businesses analyzed only the market within its own country's borders. Today, this is no longer enough. A working knowledge of and skills to compete and win in foreign markets are essential.

To take your company into the twenty-first century, to be able to meet your competition and do more than survive in the new playing field, you must take some action now.

Some will say, "It is like starting all over." This is not true. This book is about adding some building blocks to your existing foundation. It is also about what new decisions you need to make and how to make them.

It is your guide to winning in foreign markets.

And remember, "The world is your oyster." So happy harvesting.

Michele Forzley

Michele Forzley

ABOUT THE AUTHOR

Michele Forzley, managing director of Forzley & Co., your *Global Guide*® for more than 15 years, has helped businesses worldwide plan international growth and development. She holds a B.A. from Simmons College and a J.D. from the New England School of Law. Forzley & Co. is a consulting firm that offers temporary international marketing services to companies that wish an outside organization to perform research on their foreign market, develop and implement their foreign market-entry strategy, and plan international business. The company is based in New York City. She is also a speaker worldwide and an associate editor of *The Exporter* magazine.

ACKNOWLEDGMENTS

To:

Era Sapra

Vincent Lau

Olsen Securities, Inc.

The Exporter

For all their help in completing this book.

Dedication—

To Joyce Turley Nicholas for her inspiration. She has always generously given me to do and be all I can.

CONTENTS

INTRODUCTION

"A man's feet must be planted in his country,
but his eyes should survey the world."

—George Santayana

Winning in Foreign Markets: Your Global Guide® is for people who want to develop skills to tackle and succeed in foreign markets. It is intended for corporate managers, business owners, students, marketing managers, CEOs—for anyone who wants to acquire international skills and awareness.

This manual does not cover every aspect of international business. It focuses on making a commitment to conduct a new kind of business and developing a strategy to do so. It is a book about the planning you would undertake to guide your company or department in seeking new markets in foreign lands. The methods, tips and techniques have been proved in actual companies around the world. They really work.

This book also is a reference manual about information and where to find it, a key to any international strategy. It is a guide on how information is organized, where you will find it and for what purposes it can be used.

It is also universal. The methods outlined can be used by any business anywhere in the world. The steps, processes and information fit all types of economies, environments, products and services.

It is a book about how to manage the changes your business must undergo to participate in the global marketplace. The insights about the process and how to work in it will enable you to overcome obstacles and achieve success.

Your Global Guide

This book is your *Global Guide®* on how to adapt the set up of your organization and business strategy to address the realities of the global economy. This is a two-part process involving internal business planning and developing know-how about and a plan of action toward foreign markets.

To assist your efforts, numerous services are available from the public and private sector in addition to this book. These "global guides," as I call them, can assist, augment, and complement your own skills. Forzley & Co. is an example of a private-sector global guide.

Objectives for the Reader

Before you begin this book, give some thought to your goals. Place a checkmark by each goal that is especially important to you. Then use this book as your *Global Guide* to help you achieve your objectives.

I want to:

☐   **1.**   Learn about business today and for the twenty-first century.

☐   **2.**   Apply this knowledge to expand business opportunites.

☐   **3.**   Understand the steps management takes to direct a company to foreign markets.

☐   **4.**   Add value to my business.

☐   **5.**   Be able to develop and implement a plan of action.

☐   **6.**   Know where to find necessary information and training.

☐   **7.**   Increase sales and profits.

☐   **8.**   Enter new markets, expand existing markets, overcome domestic limits to growth and maintain growth.

☐   **9.**   Understand how to analyze foreign markets for any product or service.

☐   **10.**   Run a test market to refine or confirm my judgments and decisions.

☐   **11.**   Know about new levels of international law, banking and insurance.

☐   **12.**   Reap the advantages of economies of scale from global volume.

P A R T

1

Why Market in Foreign Countries?

WHY WIN IN FOREIGN MARKETS?

In 1993, world trade surpassed $8 trillion—about one-third of everything produced in the world. The volume of world trade has grown by more than 5.75 percent per year since 1984 and will continue at the same or greater rate into the twenty-first century.

Translated to your bottom line, this means foreign trade will help your company grow. If you cannot sell as much as you would like, the simple solution is to sell outside your home markets. These simple truths, plus modern technologies—the computer, digital telecommunications and long-haul jet aircraft—have fueled the growth of international trade.

Global interdependence is here to stay. In the past, you put your capital to work where it earned the best return domestically. Now, capital goods and services will flow to wherever they earn the best returns; geography and nationalism will no longer be the defining boundary.

Some countries have already learned this lesson. In Germany, Malaysia and Japan, exporting is a way of life because the local population is too small or unable to take advantage of all the country produces. In 1991, Germany ranked first in worldwide exports, boasting that one of every four jobs is in exporting.

WHY WIN IN FOREIGN MARKETS? (continued)

More Reasons to Export

Every day you wait to decide to export, foreign businesses are competing against you in your existing markets—gaining on you both on your home turf and in foreign markets where you have not begun. Every day you wait to join the global marketplace, other businesses are getting the profit you could be earning and soon you could lose the profit you are making now. Former Secretary of the U. S. Treasury Bill Simon said, "By the year 2000, there will be two types of managers, those with a global awareness and those who are unemployed."

> *Foreign trade is especially important for those who live in countries that have large foreign trade deficits. The future health of those countries depends in large part on their success in balancing the national checkbook, which includes the trade deficit. The formula is simple: when you buy more from other countries than you sell, you have a trade deficit. Balance can only come from selling more and buying less.*

This book is devoted to selling more. Your country and your business reap even more benefits than a balanced trade deficit when you sell more. The objectives for reading this book tell you what you can get. Have another look now to keep your focus on your goals while you continue to read.

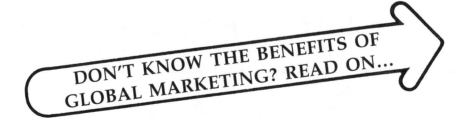

DON'T KNOW THE BENEFITS OF GLOBAL MARKETING? READ ON...

ARE FOREIGN MARKETS PROFITABLE?

The answer is a resounding YES! Almost every company today can improve sales or reduce costs of production per unit and thus benefit from foreign sales.

An average company exports about 15 percent of what it produces. Some countries export 80 percent or more of their gross national product (GNP). U.S. companies export an average of 7.5 percent of sales; about 100 U.S. companies account for more than 50 percent of all U.S. exports. In other countries, such as Germany and Japan, exports account for more than 50 percent of sales.

A clear correlation exists between exports and business health. In the United States, the only growth sector of the economy in recent years has been from those companies that exported. These same companies added staff and increased sales and profits. The companies diversified their global markets worldwide and thus were buffered from the worldwide recession.

Businesses usually fail because management neglects to plan for the future. Today, no company can begin business without looking at its market. The market is the world. Companies already in operation need to go back to the planning table and amend the business plan to add steps to tackle foreign markets.

The methods described in this book will illuminate what is different about each foreign market. Eventually, you will know which tactics will work for you everywhere and what must be changed for a specific market. The steps you take to know this important information are the same, they are the *Global Guide.*

LEARNING TO TRADE MORE EFFECTIVELY

Effective international trading has four steps:

> **STEP #1:** Decide to Commit to International Trade
>
> **STEP #2**: Develop a Market-Entry Strategy
>
> **STEP #3**: Learn Activities Necessary to International Trade
>
> **STEP #4**: Get Started and Continue to Grow

Planning Success Factors

The top management of the company must commit unequivocally to developing foreign markets. A successful strategy is just that—a strategy, a plan, an approach. What plan has ever worked without commitment?

The specifics of the commitment vary with each business. Without question, every plan requires:

► **Time** to develop and execute the plan, including gathering information and calculating a realistic timetable

► **Resources,** including information, a realistic budget, allocation of staff time or the retention of outside help

► **Recognition** that exporting is a specific business activity, separate from domestic sales, with some differing needs and yardsticks

HOW FOREIGN TRADE IS DIFFERENT

Everyone on your staff will need to learn something new. At the beginning, primarily top management, sales and marketing will be involved, since this group must do the planning. Its task is to figure out who has to learn what and assign and delegate responsibility. Fortunately, a proliferation of literature, courses and training is available. Once you itemize the what and who, finding the knowledge is the easy part. This book gives you the outline. Your job is to flesh it out.

Market-Entry Logistics

Everyone will be involved in the practicalities of foreign trade. The logistics of working with a foreign customer entail the following process:

- Finding your customer, which results from your market-entry strategy

- Negotiating and closing the deal and writing it down in an order or contract

- Processing the order

- Packaging, shipping and delivery

- Paperwork to get the order out of your country

- Paperwork to get the order into the buyer's country

- Getting paid

- Getting repeat business

You should be thinking the process is not much different from anything else you have ever done. The similarities are far greater than the differences. But you must master the differences to succeed.

Getting Started Exercise: Pick a Test Country

You will learn how to analyze a foreign market and develop your market-entry strategy. For this purpose, pick a country that you think might offer a profitable market for your business. Throughout the exercises in this book, you will analyze this country's potential and, by doing so, learn to assess the potential market of any country.

To help you apply the new skills you will learn, it will be helpful to have a few materials handy. These include:

1. Any general reference book where you can read about the country you selected. (Examples that should be in your office or home are an almanac, an encyclopedia, an atlas or book of maps.)

2. Information about the country. (Have a travel agent mail you all available material.)

3. More general information about the country and some information specific to your product or service. (To identify sources of information, have a look at the next section.) Gather three sources.

4. A telephone book.

5. A notebook or pad of paper.

6. Some file folders.

7. Pens, pencils and whatever else you use to do office paper work, including your computer or tape recorder. (If you do the exercises in this book, the answers will be a plan of action.)

SOURCES OF INFORMATION ON INTERNATIONAL TRADE

Develop a process to learn about foreign markets to identify customers.

Many resources are available to help you to understand international trade. This partial list is arranged alphabetically. Each category is multipurpose; each can be a source of information about agents, distributors, customers, suppliers, joint-venture partners and market research information. Most sources are free or nominally priced. When considering which one to use, don't underestimate the value and efficiency of buying information and remember that not any one source can address all of your questions.

For this section, have your phone book by your side as you read each category. Note the telephone numbers of any offices or companies in your locale and call to obtain the information about your target country, the organization and what it offers.

1. *Advertising:* Trade and general news publications are resources for placing your own advertisement or finding leads to follow up. There are any number of trade publications in English and in other languages. Don't stop short at the U.S. borders when looking for information, especially if you read a foreign language.

2. *Big Eight Accounting and Consulting Firms:* These are also in the information business. Because they are international, they will also have information on many countries. Often it is free, since they want your business.

3. *Commercial Banks:* Most banks have international departments staffed with informed specialists. They should be able to provide you with information in the following areas: market information, export regulations, currency exchange rates, collection of foreign receivables, letters of credit, credit information on foreign buyers, and credit-assistance programs.

4. *Your Competition:* Never underestimate what your competition will tell you. You should always consult your competitors when preparing your international marketing plan.

SOURCES OF INFORMATION (continued)

5. *Customshouse Brokers/Freight Forwarders:* These businesses move goods into and out of the country. Each is a private service company, licensed to assist importers or exporters move their goods. They prepare forms, pay duties, arrange for shipping and delivery—in short, they are invaluable sources of detailed information on duties, controls, and restrictions on the movement of goods and methods of shipping and documentation.

6. *Databases:* On-line databases are proliferating. Computer literacy is a must for the twenty-first century. Any computer or magazine store can direct you to databases that are relevant to your industry.

7. *Directories:* Specialized business directories list information about companies in international business. They include: Marconi's International Register, Dun and Bradstreet's Principal International Business, American Export Register, and Moody's International. Publications such as these list both U.S. and foreign companies that export and import. Generally quite expensive, the books are categorized alphabetically by product and company name. Start in the library to familiarize yourself with these sources.

8. *Educational Institutions:* Most universities and colleges have educational programs on international trade at both degree and nondegree levels. Offerings range from one-day seminars to extensive courses designed for business people. Some aspects of international trade, such as documentation and letters of credit, are quite detailed and are well suited to study at the university level.

9. *Foreign Commercial Attachés:* All countries that have diplomatic relations with your country have an embassy in your capital which employs a foreign commerical attaché whose job is to promote trade between his or her country and yours.

10. *International Trade Consultants:* Trade consultants usually specialize by industry, product, region or country. They offer services such as developing a market-entry strategy, researching the market to locate joint-venture partners, conducting feasibility studies, helping to establish foreign branches and providing information on local laws and regulations. Forzley & Co. in New York is an example.

11. *Libraries:* Your local library's business branch will have many books on aspects of international trade. Don't overlook this useful source. For example, directories are found in libraries. Libraries also keep domestic and foreign newspapers on file.

12. *Networking:* Learn to network everywhere so you can expand your contacts, build relationships, develop resources, multiply options, increase profits and advance your career and business.

13. *Nongovernmental Organizations (NGOs):* NGOs collect and publish various reports. For example, the United Nations publishes a statistical and demographic yearbook and many other works. So do the International Monetary Fund, the Office of Economic and Cultural Development, the General Agreement on Tariffs and Trade, World Bank, Asian Development Bank, InterAmerican Development Bank, and the European Community. These are available from libraries and the organizations themselves. Remember that these organizations also fund certain projects that provide market opportunites.

14. *Periodicals:* *Business International, The Monitor, Business Week, Asia Week, The Exporter, Forbes, The Economist* and many other business periodicals publish regular and special reports.

15. *The State Department and/or Foreign Ministry:* The State Department is not responsible for promoting trade; the Department of Commerce or the Ministry of Trade and Industry performs this function. The State Department does, however, implement certain foreign policy decisions through the use of regulations that do affect international business. These rules can restrict certain imports and exports for foreign-policy reasons. If your product or service is subject to any controls, consult a lawyer on how to manage the sale of your product.

16. *State or Local Municipal Governments:* State export-development programs are growing rapidly to help local economies flourish. Programs include export education, marketing assistance, market development, trade missions and shows. Call your local or state representative to inquire about these programs.

17. *Trade Fairs and Shows:* A trade fair is an exhibition by a country or region of products by producers, trade associations, chambers of commerce or government trade-promotion departments. There are all sorts of trade fairs around the world. You can visit shows as a buyer or you can exhibit and sell your product. Shows provide a great opportunity to inspect your competition. All commercial attaches can tell you when trade shows are scheduled in their country. Selling at trade shows is a special type of marketing that can be extremely effective. Learn the techniques of trade-show selling before joining a trade show.

SOURCES OF INFORMATION (continued)

18. *Trade Missions:* A trade mission enables you to visit a foreign country and have prearranged customized meetings with potential trading partners. The function of a trade mission is to match local people to you. You say to the mission director, "I want to sell footballs," and the job of the trade mission director is to find you buyers of footballs. You also receive broad information about doing business in that country. This is a very efficient way to enter a foreign market for the first time.

19. *Trade Organizations:* Business has organized itself into various trade groups, either by product or geographic region. We are all familiar with chambers of commerce and other trade associations. These same organizations often have an international division. Most importantly, similar organizations exist in all countries. Trade organizations are great repositories of information and people with whom to do business. All have international programs and services. They offer trade missions and seminars, and are fruitful sources of networking opportunities.

20. *Departments of Commerce or Ministries of Trade:* The Commerce Department is the national agency of the government responsible for assisting business. Many countries have commercial attachés located in their foreign embassies. The commercial section is there to help you do business in that country. The function operates out of the Department of Commerce, although technically the embassy is part of the State Department. Commercial sections often keep literature about local enterprises, keep directories, know who's who in those places, how to do business there, and what information will help you find out about the local economy. You should check into the commercial section when you visit any foreign country.

21. *World Trade Centers:* In many cities, some 65 world trade center offices exist around the world. They are part of the World Trade Centers Association. Some local business people have gotten together and set up these resource places for businesses. They operate much like trade associations. The Twin Towers in New York is an example.

What is available in your home town? Your state? Your national government? The government of your target?

P A R T

2

Introducing
Your *Global Guide*

YOUR *GLOBAL GUIDE* TO SUCCESS

Looking at a market involves screening lots of information. Must you now become an amateur economist, sociologist, political scientist and cultural anthropologist? The answer is yes! Remember, these disciplines are not sciences. Their use and application is far less rigid than you might think. In fact, whether you have been in business for any length of time or are brand new, you have already learned a great deal about the screening process.

Winning in foreign markets results from a conscientious and systematic examination of the factors and ingredients that make a market. Then comes a planned implementation of your strategy. You don't start into a country where there is no market.

What follows is your *Global Guide*. It is just that—a guide that you adapt to fit your specific product and/or service and your company. Winning in foreign markets is not one-size-fits-all; it is tailor-made. The balance of this book is your opportunity to customize this method.

Getting Ready

As you survey the world, you are deciding whether to sell your product in a country and how to do so. The first rule to remember:

Swim only in pools that have water!

Clearly, there are many people in the former Soviet Union—a great deal of unmet consumer need and want. The problem is that there is not much water in the pool. Because of a poor economy, changes from communist state to private economies and political turmoil, neither the people nor the governments have much money. It's hard to get paid.

Getting paid is only one element of deciding the pool contains water. "Is there a market?" may seem like a simple question, but many factors comprise the answer. This chapter lists and discusses these factors. Impediments to market entry (including tariffs or import duties, local regulations on products and labeling, and health and safety laws) also determine how much water is in the pool. This section helps suggest what swimming strokes to use to win the race.

INGREDIENTS FOR SUCCESS

Brand

The ingredients that follow are also useful in determining other questions as well, such as the four Ps of marketing (price, product, placement and promotion), what entry method to use, measuring the depth of the market and understanding what aspects of culture affect your strategy. Take your time in examining each ingredient. Each has a multiple purpose as you plan your strategy to win foreign markets.

INGREDIENTS

Macroeconomic Factors

Infrastructure and Physical Features

Political Forces

Risk Considerations

Microeconomic Components

Financial Conditions

Socioeconomic Elements

Sociocultural Influences

Legal Aspects

Labor Issues

MACROECONOMIC FACTORS

This category sketches the overall health of the country and level of development. You can think of it as the "ripeness" index, because markets have a readiness quality. You may decide a country is not ready for your company now, but return to it later.

This basic dimension includes several questions leading to the most important question:

Does the Country Have Enough People and Resources to Buy Your Product or Service?

The dimensions to investigate are:

1. What is the gross domestic product (GDP) per capita?

This rough guide tells you how much money the average citizen has to spend. Compare the GDP per capita of India ($350) to Denmark ($20,510). If you sell VCRs or another sophisticated electronic device, Denmark would be a better market even though India has a much larger population.

2. What does the country produce? Who buys it? What does it not produce? Where does it get it?

Every country has some or all of the basic industries or activities that provide what its people need for personal and industrial use. The list below includes some basic industries. Which ones does your target country have? Try to find out what shape your own industry is in in your target country.

Manufacturing
Construction
Health
Power generation
Telecommunications
Mining or natural resource exploitation
Advertising or public relations

Food
Transportation
Education
Military
Imports and Exports
Agriculture, chief crops and livestock

MACROECONOMIC FACTORS (continued)

3. How is income distributed and what are personal consumption patterns?

Are large segments of the population poor? Look at who does and does not hold the wealth of the country. In advanced nations, income is distributed more evenly. In developing nations, greater income inequality will exist. This tendency will reverse as the nation progresses. Look as well at the percentage of income that is available for discretionary spending.

> *Example: Costa Rica is a country where 20 percent of the population receives 50 percent of the national income. With a population of about 3.12 million, this is a sizable group of luxury-goods buyers.*

4. How much private investment is there?

This ratio is that part of national income allocated to increasing the nation's productive capacity. New investment increases GNP and employment, signals a growing market, foretells of a favorable investment climate and most importantly tells you that the local government enjoys the confidence of the business community.

Exercise: Chart the Macroeconomics of Your Target

From the literature you have about the country you have selected, fill in the answers. First write down the impression you now have as to whether you believe there is a market for your product or service. This is not a final conclusion. It is a first impression.

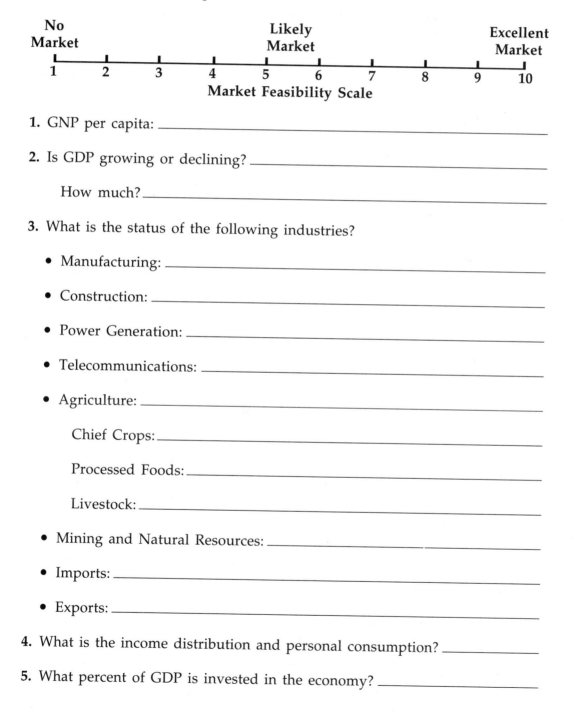

1. GNP per capita: _____

2. Is GDP growing or declining? _____

   How much? _____

3. What is the status of the following industries?

   • Manufacturing: _____

   • Construction: _____

   • Power Generation: _____

   • Telecommunications: _____

   • Agriculture: _____

      Chief Crops: _____

      Processed Foods: _____

      Livestock: _____

   • Mining and Natural Resources: _____

   • Imports: _____

   • Exports: _____

4. What is the income distribution and personal consumption? _____

5. What percent of GDP is invested in the economy? _____

INFRASTRUCTURE AND PHYSICAL FEATURES

Surface features in a country, such as mountains; plains; waterways; climate; the kind and quantity of natural resources, including oil, water, minerals and timber; and infrastructure elements such as roads, bridges, telecommunications facilities and power availability all help determine the economic strength of a country.

A country's location explains its political and trade relationships. Proximity has been—and always will be—a major reason to trade and to form trade groupings. The European Community is a perfect example of this principle.

Topography can help or hinder trade. Mountains can be barriers. In Spain, the mountains created five distinct regions, each with a different culture and language. The Amazon jungle or the Congo, while wealthy with natural resources, are almost impassable.

Inland waterways and ports of entry, on the other hand, offer not only water for consumption, but also passages easing travel and delivery of goods. The development of Europe as a great trading block was substantially aided by the extensive inland waterways, especially the Rhine River. In the United States it was the Mississippi; for China the Yangtze; and in Holland the port of Rotterdam.

Natural resources include vital energy sources such as oil, coal, or wood. Natural resources also include water, a population large enough to support the work necessary to sustain the economy, arable land, fresh air, and indigenous flora and fauna. Unfortunately, we now also have to consider the degree of pollution contamination as a factor.

Climate sets limits on what people can do physically both by themselves and with the natural resources a country offers. Climate is also important for product mix.

Exercise: Infrastructure Assessment

1. Describe five key physical features of your target country.

   1. _____

   2. _____

   3. _____

   4. _____

   5. _____

2. What topographical features, if any, are important to your product or service?

_____

_____

3. Research the following infrastructure features of your target country. Place a checkmark if the condition of each item will help or hinder your efforts to market in that country.

Help   *Hinder*

☐   ☐   Roads

☐   ☐   Airports

☐   ☐   Railway Systems

☐   ☐   Ports/Harbors

☐   ☐   Telecommunications

☐   ☐   Electricity/Power/Fuel

POLITICAL FORCES

Politics is as important as topography. Thanks to modern television broadcasting, we all can see the impact politics have on the lives of people everywhere.

Politics and ideologies reflect the local laws, their interpretations and enforcement. Political forces can be ideological, secular or based in religion. Some ideologies you may encounter include:

- Communism

- Socialism

- Tribalism

- Capitalism

- Democracy

- Islam

- Monarchy

The particular ideology of a country tells you **who** is your customer; it may only be the government in a socialist state. It tells you **what** kinds of political risks may be presented to you, such as violence or any abrupt change of power, or the possibilities of nationalization, privatization or terrorism.

No country is pure in its ideology. Therefore, every country will present a blend and spectrum of degrees of varying ideologies. Witness Russia and former East Germany as these countries move from total communism and state-run economies to democracy and privately held businesses. Contrast Latin America, where the governments have held major industries such as telecommunication, oil production and others and are now privatizing these industries. Historically, governments have held so-called strategic industries and are now leaving them to the private sector to operate more efficiently.

Exercise: Assess the Political Climate

1. Describe the political and ideological picture of your target country.

_____

_____

2. What is the dominant "ism"?

_____

_____

3. Who is the customer there?

_____

_____

4. What risks from politics do you foresee?

_____

_____

RISK CONSIDERATIONS

The type of information you will need to judge the risks of a country will vary with the type of business you are doing and the length of time required for your company to realize a return on its investment into the market.

You can do an analysis yourself, hire a company to do it or buy an existing report from some of the sources listed earlier. The following is one method of comparing countries and is based on a composite analysis.

A GLOBAL RATING OF VARIOUS RISKS				
Based on a *Wall Street Journal* report, 9/20/91: On a 1–100 Scale				
Country	Political Safety	Financial Safety	Economic Safety	Average
Switzerland	93.0	50.0	39.5	91.5
U.S.	78.0	49.0	39.5	83.5
Malaysia	71.0	45.0	88.5	77.5
Mexico	71.0	41.0	28.5	70.5
Your target _____				

On a scale where 100 is the safest, Switzerland clearly wins. If safety were your only concern, you could stop here. But if you are selling a product sold in volume, would Switzerland be the best market?

Assign values to your target county for its relative riskiness.

Country	Political Risk	Financial	Economic	Average

International Risks

To understand any market, one must grasp the relationship the country has with the rest of the world. Every country today is affected by the events in the rest of the world. This is called the global ripple effect. We all remember the Organization of Petroleum Exporting Countries (OPEC) oil price increases and the 1986 oil price collapse. Interest rates and inflation were affected everywhere.

MICROECONOMIC COMPONENTS

Macroeconomic factors tell you about the whole economy. Next, have a look at the industry in which your product or service fits.

Gather information on the larger category of industry in which your company fits. You may find the following questions helpful.

► Does the country produce the product locally? _____

_____

► What is the national consumption? _____

_____

► Does the country now import the product? _____

_____

► If so, from where? How much? _____

_____

► What percent of national consumption does this represent? _____

_____

► Are there plans to produce locally in the future? _____

_____

► Is local production possible? _____

_____

► What economic characteristics are necessary before this country will buy your product? _____

_____

► Is the market growing? Shrinking? Remaining stable? _____

_____

MICROECONOMIC COMPONENTS (continued)

Now again ask yourself your impression, does my company have a market in this country?

Competition, Distribution and Market Share

These issues are important to understanding your market. You know what competition is. Now look at the target country and learn what competition you would face there from local companies and from other countries. What are they selling? What price, quality, etc.? To determine if there is a market, and how to plan to enter it, you will need to look at competition.

Distribution is part of the marketing mix:

- Can your product be distributed in the country?

- What is currently available as a method of distribution?

- Is it the same or different from your home market?

A favorite example is the U.S. "do it yourself" market. Few places in the world have the kind of buy-anything-to-fix-it stores that the United States enjoys. Can you afford to construct a distribution system? While you need not resolve this question of how will you get the product into the hands of the customer now, part of the answer to the question, "Do I have a market at all?" is found by looking at existing distribution methods.

Look at your target country to identify foreign and local competition.

- How has it addressed the distribution issue?

_____

_____

- Can you achieve a large enough market share to make the effort worth your time and money?

_____

_____

By now, you may have found a feature of your target country that gives you the impression there is no market. If this is the case, pick another country for the purpose of the exercises in this book. If so far, your impression is positive, remember it is still an impression. The purpose of these exercises is to give you a methodology to look at any foreign market. Until you finish the analysis, you may miss information critical to a correct conclusion.

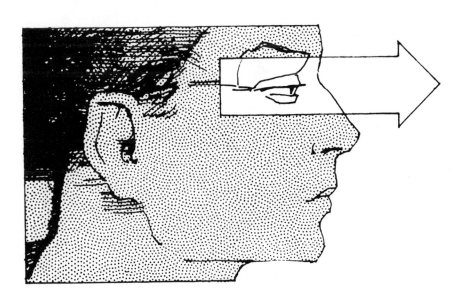

FINANCIAL CONDITIONS

The financial condition of a country means more than whether you will get paid. Of course, unless you are a charitable organization, making money is the essence of doing business. At this point in the analysis, there are other questions to address.

Exercise: What's the Financial Picture?

How easily can the customer convert from local currency to your currency?

_____

Is countertrade, barter or another noncash payment method required for some or all of payment? _____

What is the exchange rate? _____

- Free market? _____
- Black market? _____

- Fixed? _____
- Two- or more-tiered? _____

What is the local regulatory environment for currency? _____

Is capital freely movable from outside into and inside out of the country?

_____

What is the national balance of payments?

- National debt? _____

- International debt? _____

- Balance of trade? _____

What kind of documentation is required to move money? _____

_____

What tariffs and duties are due on the goods or services you sell? _____

_____

What are the monetary and fiscal policies of the government? _____
_____

- Is inflation under control? _____

Again, what is your impression? Do you have a market? In addition to addressing this question of whether your company has a market, you will be developing other points to keep in mind about the market. For example, the amount of import duty the customer will pay will affect the price. Do you have to determine an export price for your product that is different from your domestic price?

List three other points to consider that are important to your company:

1. _____

2. _____

3. _____

SOCIOECONOMIC ELEMENTS

Socioeconomic factors represent information about the physical attributes of a population. Some companies have launched long-term strategies based on population figures. For example, Whirlpool bought foreign appliance manufacturing businesses between 1988–1991 to be able to manufacture in 11 countries and to distribute in 45 countries outside the United States. The company chose countries that had young populations—i.e., people who were going to get married, set up households and have babies and thus would need washers, dryers and refrigerators.

Find answers for your target country to answer the following questions:

1. What is the total population? _____

2. What is the ratio of population growth to rate of GDP growth? _____

_____

A GDP growth rate rising faster than population rate is preferable.

3. What is the age distribution? _____
Developed countries tend to have more older people; developing countries have more younger people. This characteristic affects not only what people buy, but also how much discretionary income and purchasing power they have.

4. What is the status of women and birth control? _____

_____

Educated women have fewer babies and wait longer to do so. They also work and therefore have less time. These factors affect GNP and population growth. Working women also value convenience!

5. What is the population density? _____

_____

We are seeing a shift from rural to urban lifestyles in the world today. This influences the method and cost of distributing goods, as well as what marketing methods can be used.

6. Other factors:

- Divorce rates: _____

- Number of working women: _____

No Market				Likely Market					Excellent Market
1	2	3	4	5	6	7	8	9	10

Socioeconomic Feasibility Scale

Your impression:

List three socio-economic factors important for your company to remember:

1. _____

2. _____

3. _____

DO YOU KNOW THE LOCAL CULTURE OF YOUR TARGET COUNTRY?

SOCIOCULTURAL INFLUENCES

These forces not only tell us about our macromarket, but are very important to understanding our customers! Some people will tell you that the most important factor in international trade is culture, and that a cultural gaffe will kill any deal. Learning about the local culture is essential to any market-entry strategy. Fortunately, enough information is available so you can arm yourself and avoid blunders. You also must learn about the culture to gain the total picture of whether your business has a market, and how you will approach the market and your customer.

Culture: The sum total beliefs, rules, techniques, institutions and artifacts that characterize a population. Culture can be broken down into many categories. They include:

- Social and business etiquette

- History

- Folklore

- Current affairs

- Relations between your country and theirs

- Values (national sources of pride, artists, sports figures or teams)

- Religion

- Political structure

- Practical matters (attitude, time, hours of business, currency)

- Aesthetics (art, drama, music, folklore, dances, color and its meanings, architecture)

- Education

- Material culture (how things are made, what is made and why)

- Language: the number of national languages

- Ethnic composition

- Social organizations

Every society considers its culture superior to others. Culture is learned by the members of a group who use their culture to define their boundaries. The elements of culture are interrelated.

You may be thinking, "I don't have time to be a social anthropologist. I just want to sell my products." Keep in mind two things. The first is that without realizing it, you are absorbing facts about culture while learning about a market. This section is designed to have you focus on the details of culture, because one or more may have significant impact on your ability to sell. Culture affects marketing mix and how you manage your personnel.

Did You Know?

> ► The smell of lemon means death in the Philippines. Lemon-fresh soap will not sell there.
>
> ► In Japan, only prostitutes recline in public. If you are selling beds, you would not show someone testing it out in your advertising.
>
> ► In Latin America, the attitude toward authority demands that the boss be the boss. Modern methods of management will not work.
>
> ► Protestants, Confucians, and Shintos all believe it is one's duty to glorify God by hard work.

Describe the cultural characteristics of your test market and identify the three most important elements of the culture that affect the market for your product.

The three most important cultural characteristics are:

1. _____

2. _____

3. _____

LEGAL ASPECTS

There are five aspects of the law with which to concern yourself.

1. **The laws of the target country** regarding import duties and quotas; intellectual property rights; and local regulations with which you must comply, such as packaging and labeling, content descriptions, safety and health regulations and other standards such as product liability issues. Generally, the same issues that affect your product in your own country affect your product elsewhere.

   Find information for the following for your target country:

   a. Taxation, duties _____

   b. Quotas _____

   c. Warranties _____

   d. Packaging _____

   e. Labeling _____

   f. Use of local language _____

   g. Measurement systems, metric or English _____

   h. Quarantines _____

   i. Border checks (e.g., for agricultural products) _____

   j. Specialty items, such as goods used by the military or municipalities, toxic or dangerous goods, or items subject to luxury taxes

   _____

2. **International law;** that is, the body of law that has evolved as the law that governs activity between citizens from different countries. Most of us are familiar with it in the form of treaties, such as the North American Free Trade Agreement (NAFTA) or the European Economic Community (EEC). Treaties supersede local laws. Treaties determine the contracts you use, what local laws do not apply and how you resolve disputes.

3. **The laws of your country of origin** affect your operations outside your country. Consider everything from exchange controls, taxes on foreign income, accounting for foreign business and how you do business outside the country. Some countries, including the United States, have laws like the Foreign Corrupt Practices Act (FCPA), which prohibits bribery or payoffs to government officials. In other countries, bribery is a matter of course. *Your citizenship holds you to the laws of your own country, even if you are on foreign shores.* It is not allowable to do something that is illegal in your home even though you are in another country.

] bribery?

4. **The laws you make** govern each part of your transaction. While we do not think of the terms and conditions we agree to in contracts as "law," they are in fact so. When we consent to be bound by these terms, they become laws that we make. When we think of the elements of the order process, negotiating, agreeing, signing, packing, shipping, insuring, delivery, and getting paid, we see that for each step, we must make different agreements.

Try to list all the people or organizations that are part of each step. For example, getting paid involves one or more banks and, of course, the buyer; shipping and delivery involve the transportation provider and others.

People and organizations with whom I will interact and make agreements are: _____

_____

_____

_____

LEGAL ASPECTS (continued)

5. **Last, your company or industry can have standards of its own to apply everywhere.** For example, U.S. toy manufacturers employ U.S. toy safety rules in making toys, even though the toys are not made in or necessarily sold in the United States. The standards of your industry may be higher than those of your markets, and you can meet them. Or the contrary may be true—your standards may be lower than the foreign or international standards, in which case you will have to rise to the occasion.

What are the standards of my industry?

_____

My company?

_____

Do they apply worldwide?

_____

Does my trade association have this information?

_____

LABOR ISSUES

Labor is an issue for two kinds of market-entry strategies: It is most important for those setting up a facility in another country. It is also important for those acting through an agent or other local representative to avoid an undesirable employer-employee relationship. In the latter situation, you must understand the labor situation to know the field of possibilities and to select the best local representative.

For your target country, find information for these issues:

- The quality, quantity and mobility of labor:

  _____

- Legal restrictions and requirements, including labor unions:

  _____

- The costs of labor, wages, commissions, benefits and training:

  _____

- Culture (again):

  _____

Does the labor situation affect my company domestically? _____

In my target country? _____

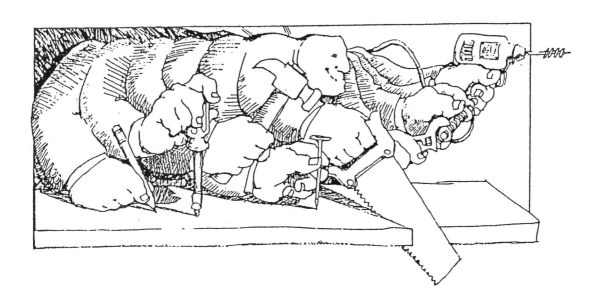

P A R T

3

Aspects of International Marketing

STICK TO THE BASICS— REMEMBER THE FOUR Ps

Brand.

1. **PRODUCT:** What will you sell?

2. **PRICE:** Will the price be the same or different as for domestic sales?

3. **PROMOTION:** How will you communicate to the market that your product is available?

4. **PLACEMENT:** How will you distribute the product?

The four Ps of marketing are probably not foreign to you. They are part of any marketing course. If you have not had a marketing course, perhaps you should consider stopping here and picking up a book about marketing.*

While studying it, focus on how you have resolved these principles for your domestic sales.

This section will generally review these principles and draw your attention to what may be different for your international sales. Look at your domestic business as if it is completely separate. Use it as a frame of reference to chart the four Ps for your foreign sales.

WHAT ARE YOU SELLING?

---

*For a helpful book, read *Writing and Implementing a Marketing Plan*, by Richard F. Gerson, Menlo Park, CA: Crisp, 1991.

1. PRODUCT

The answer to "What are you selling?" is core for any business. Your existing product or service will certainly be a starting point for the choice you make. Some companies sell the same product in foreign markets that they do domestically. Some sell a totally different product. Others sell a variation of the basic product.

You can only decide what to sell by looking at a specific market and considering the method of growth your company has selected. The characteristics of a market will partially clarify the answer; this is the external information and influence with which a company must deal. Another component of the decision is internal and has to do with your growth strategy. Selling products in foreign markets is a growth strategy. To grow, a company can diversify its product lines, increase the size of its market share and/or quantity of its markets or move production closer to customers.

While considering "What are you selling?" we are not looking at the decision to diversify a product line. Many decisions beyond the scope of this book are involved in that decision. We are looking at the question of whether your product needs to be adapted to suit a foreign market.

An example is Coca Cola. We all know the total product: a red-and-white can and a sweet drink. It is a combination of a physical product and a brand name. The physical product is known worldwide, but it is different for different markets. It is adapted for varying local taste buds, even within a country. The brand name is the same worldwide, although it is written in local languages. As an experiment on your next trip, taste a Coke and see whether it is different from what you get at home. You may also notice other differences, such as can size and whether you can get Diet Coke or other flavors. These differences result from conscious choices by Coca Cola as it has answered the question of "What are we selling?"

Consumer products will be subject to the most variables, in terms of the physical product and the associated message it carries. Soap is a basic product in some countries; in others it is given in a fancy box as a gift and the message is quite different. Industrial products and services are at the other end of the spectrum and are not adapted as much, if at all, since change is not necessary. A ball bearing is a ball bearing no matter who buys it.

What Are You Selling?

1. What are you selling? A product or a service? _____

_____

2. Is it a consumer or industrial product? _____

3. Do you presently adapt your product for different market segments? If so, how? Will it be different for your target market? _____

_____

4. Describe the physical product: _____

Packaging _____

Brand name _____

Accessories _____

Serviceability _____

Warranties _____

Size, shape, color _____

5. What else does my customer get with my product? _____

_____

Keep in mind that your answers will be again modified as we look at the rest of the four Ps and the potential impact your product will make on another culture. Now also look back at the ingredients of the target market and see if any of the observations you made are important to incorporate into the decision of "What are you selling?"

2. PRICE

Perhaps the most difficult yet important question to answer is at what price should you sell your product? The answer is more than the sum of cost and mark-up. Price is a controllable variable. Your choice of price will help you achieve your marketing objective.

Setting a high price reinforces the promotional objective that emphasizes quality. A low price can be used to achieve market share or other goal. Price can maximize the perceived value of the product to the customer. Price also determines other choices, such as what will be production run, sizes and dates; what will middlemen be paid and whether you run afoul of pricing regulations.

When considering what price to charge for exports, again consider the same factors that you reviewed for the "**what** are you selling?" section. If your policy and product are of the type to be standardized rather than adapted, your pricing will be standardized too and the price in all foreign markets will be the same.

Consider now what type of pricing you may use.

Another question to consider is whether your price will be the same internationally as it is for domestic sales. Generally, the answer is no. An export price is often less because the ultimate customer must absorb the costs of transporting the goods to and within the country and the costs of the local representative who will want his share. Thus, the exporter charges less. The amount may well be less than or the same as for large domestic wholesale purchasers.

A company can have a price for sales from a foreign location to customers within the country; this price is called **foreign national pricing.** It is, of course, a domestic price within the country, but foreign as to your head office.

Watch out for the local rules on:

- Price controls

- Fixed prices for certain goods

- Minimum sales prices

- Prohibitions on discounts

- Your competitors' prices

Two other points to keep in mind are the impact of labor unions in a foreign land and the product's life cycle. This cycle may vary from country to country and, therefore, the pricing selected will have to be adjusted accordingly.

What is your domestic pricing structure? _____

_____

What is your price for export? What impact does the destination have on price? What impact does the projected increase on volume have on the price?

_____

_____

Will you be manufacturing or assembling in a foreign location and, if so, what will be the price in that location? _____

_____

A word about transfer pricing: Transfer prices can be used to circumvent currency restrictions or reduce income taxes to a home country. Many countries, however, have tax rules that seek to stop you from using transfer pricing to avoid local taxes. But where possible, and in a manner consistent with your tax requirements, use this method. It works as follows:

Transfer Pricing

Great Britain	Jamaica	United States
• Item X is produced for $100 • Corporate tax rate on profit is 52% • Item X is sold to Jamaican subsidiary for $100 • No profit was made on sale • No profit = No tax	• Item X is resold to a subsidiary for $200 • Corporate tax rate on profit is 5% • $200 – $100 = $100 • $100 × 5% = $5 • Tax paid: $5	• Item X is sold at cost: $200 • Corporate tax rate on profit is 34% • No profit earned • No profit = No tax

3. PROMOTION

Closely aligned with what you are selling is the subject of promotion. Promotion mix includes promotional strategy, advertising, public relations and selling method.

Promotional strategy has six common choices:

1. **Same product—same message**
   Avon products are the same worldwide and offer the same message of beauty.

2. **Same product—different message**
   Schweppes drinks. Some markets target Schweppes as a mixer with gin; elsewhere the drink is marketed as a cold, refreshing soft drink.

3. **Product adaptation—message adaptation**
   Tang is the breakfast drink of Americans and astronauts; in Latin America it is a drink to have during the day.

4. **Product adaptation—same message**
   Personal soap is ordinary for America and Europe, but for some cultures it is suitable as a gift.

5. **Different product—same message**
   Manually operated washing machines are a low-priced product to wash clothes.

6. **Different product for the same use—different message**
   Welding torches for developing countries offer employment opportunities, whereas automatic welding machines for industrialized countries offer mechanized labor.

Which strategy do you now use? Why? _____

_____

Which one will you use for your target market? Why? _____

_____

ADVERTISING AND PUBLIC RELATIONS

Advertising and public relations happen to be one of America's greatest export products. For Americans, the standards are familiar; thus, the selection of an advertising and PR plan will be relatively easy.

Advertising is simply a paid, nonpersonal presentation of ideas, goods or services by your company. The kind of ad; the choice of media; how much to spend; what kinds of goals you want to achieve (product recognition or lead generation, a local or global approach); and whether you employ a managed centralized or regional decision-making or international standardization approach are some of the questions to address. A reputable advertising agency that has foreign offices will be able to assist you in addressing these issues.

Public relations is a method of communicating with your company's public to secure a favorable impression of the company or product. PR firms are available to construct and implement a PR plan or you can do one yourself. A PR plan includes press coverage of your firm's activities, including newspaper or magazine articles, radio announcements, company sponsorship of local events or other activities, all or some of which may be useful to your goals.

What advertising and public relations practices do you now use? _____

_____

Why did you choose them? _____

_____

What will you use for your target foreign market? _____

_____

What are you currently basing this choice on? _____

_____

4. PLACEMENT

Sales approaches are the methods you or your local representative use to sell. On the next page, you will select one of the market-entry strategies available for foreign sales. Your choice will reflect which selling approach is appropriate for your product or service and how your product can be distributed in the foreign market.

Distribution involves the physical logistics of getting the product to the customer. It is a function of both the entry strategy and selling approach your product requires.

Primary sales approaches include:

Executive selling: High-ticket items and long-term contracts, usually greater than $50,000, are sold by the chief executive or vice-president whose involvement is necessary to win the potential customer's trust. This category includes major medical equipment, consulting or engineering services.

In-house sales force: This team conducts telemarketing activity or sells products that support the cost of sales. Such items include electronic instrumentation and industrial cleaning contracts.

Sales representatives: These are usually manufacturers' representatives, brokers, wholesalers, distributors, or other commissioned and part-time sales people. They usually represent other companies and are most often used to sell products priced between $1,000 and $10,000 per item, including foods, flooring and software.

Mass distribution: This category includes retailing, direct-mail and telemarketing for products that sell for less than $1,000. This method is the most competitive and must be carefully planned. Examples of items include consumer products and magazine subscriptions.

Which selling approach do you presently use? Why? _____

_____

Which approach will you use for your target country? Why? _____

_____

SELECT A MARKET-ENTRY STRATEGY

There are only six possibilities. One or more will work for you in a given country and you may use different methods for different countries. Which one you select will depend on the size of your existing staff, the type of product you are selling and, of course, the selling approach that is right for your product.

Market Entry Strategies

► **DIRECT SALES**

► **AGENTS**

► **DISTRIBUTORS**

► **SALES TO GOVERNMENTS**

► **FOREIGN OPERATIONS**

► **JOINT VENTURES AND STRATEGIC ALLIANCES**

What method(s) does your company use now for domestic sales? _____

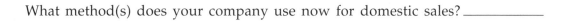

(DIRECT SALES)

Direct sales are common and should always be used. Here, the home office directs actions through the use of telephone, FAX, telex and advertising or other lead-generation methods, such as direct mail. The head office makes the sale to the customer and ships the order. This type of sale requires a staff with the tools to sell in this manner. Of course, a plan to generate leads and prospects is also necessary. For many products and countries, it is possible to obtain prospect lists or create leads through direct-marketing methods. This is called "exporting from your desk" or "arm-chair exporting."*

---

*Copyright of Land Grant & Associates

MARKET-ENTRY STRATEGIES (continued)

Included in direct sales are export management companies (EMCs) and export trading companies (ETCs). EMCs are separate businesses that conduct export transactions for other companies. This type of business usually does all exporting work for its clients and often specializes in a particular product or industry. The manufacturer may continue domestic sales or not, but leaves the exporting to the EMC. Usually, the EMC does not take title to the product, but arranges the paperwork.

ETCs do the same as EMCs, except they often take title and pay you an agreed-upon amount. Some ETCs offer some consulting services to your company.

Generally, both ETCs and EMCs are valuable methods to sell a product. They will distribute your product worldwide and take the burden of the work from you. You, of course, lose the experience and the opportunity to keep your finger on the pulse of your foreign markets. As a result, you may not make as much profit as you would if you sold yourself. Moreover, you depend on the EMC or ETC, which may or may not do a good job. You will have less of an opportunity of knowing what is possible unless you study the matter yourself.

How do you conduct direct sales now? _____

_____

What process do you use for domestic sales? _____

Can your staff do more? _____

(AGENTS)

Agents are commissioned salespeople. All of us are familiar with the use of agents to represent companies. It is a common strategy in a foreign country because it is an efficient and low-cost way of entering a market. For some products and customers (for example, sales to governments) sometimes an agent is required. This method also provides a local contact for the customer.

Agents do not take ownership of the products. They merely find customers and take orders. You will have more luck with an agent if you identify your agent's:

✓ Profile ✓ Other principals

✓ Experience ✓ Potential customers

✓ Education ✓ Reputation

Also, look at what will you do to support your agent:

☐ Offer training on your product

☐ Visit prospects so the agent learns the sale

☐ Provide in-country sales seminars

☐ Develop literature customized to the culture

How often will you visit? _____

What will you pay your agent?

☐ Straight commission?

☐ Draw against commission?

Will the agent have an exclusive territory? yes _____ no _____

What will you require of the agent?

☐ Sales reports?

☐ That he or she not represent a competitor?

How will you end the relationship? _____

Will it have a term? yes _____ no _____

MARKET-ENTRY STRATEGIES (continued)

AGENT'S PROFILE AND AGREEMENT

Generally it is also advisable to have a written memo of your agreement. Make sure that you check local rules on whether you have to register the agency and rules on ending it. Some countries have definite rules on both.

Write a profile of your agent. _____

_____

_____

_____

_____

What will you do to support your agent? _____

_____

_____

_____

_____

(DISTRIBUTORS)

The difference between a distributor and an agent is that a distributor buys from you and sells out of its inventory.

A classic example of a distributor is the local auto dealership. It is a separate business under the distributor's name, selling a certain make of auto. The dealer buys autos from the manufacturer at a deep discount and resells them to the public. The dealer generally is bound to follow the manufacturer's advertising, sales promotions and methods of selling and must keep and use the manufacturer's trade name. A distributor maintains a territory and generally has exclusivity over it.

Sometimes a distributor buys to repackage under its own name. This method of selling is known as private label. It is frequently used for international sales.

The same questions you have asked about agents, you may want to ask about distributors. In addition, you may wish to consider:

- Will you require the distributor to purchase a minimum annual amount?

- Will you charge an initial distributor fee?

- Will you charge a monthly amount?

- What else will you require the distributor to do?
  —Attend trade shows
  —Collect market intelligence
  —Register the company trademark

- What sales terms will you allow the distributor to offer?

- What support will you offer your distributors?
  —Advertising
  —Promotional
  —Literature

Please note that there are some legal questions for both agents and distributors that require special caution. You certainly do not want the agent or distributor to be considered your employee. Foreign local law will govern this question.

MARKET-ENTRY STRATEGIES (continued)

More important, however, is the ability of your agent or distributor to obligate your company to any sort of commitment. The way to avoid this problem is to address it clearly with your representative and specifically state this point in the contract between you.

Describe how you will work with your distributor. _____

_____

_____

_____

_____

_____

_____

_____

_____

SALES TO GOVERNMENTS

Sales to governments are so specialized and have such extraordinary aspects that they deserve a category unto themselves.

It is included in this chapter, even though it is not really an entry strategy, to acknowledge that a foreign government can be a major customer. In some countries, the government is the only customer possible. Think of the former Soviet Union. Today, the number of countries in which this is the case is dwindling. Rather, you will find that governments are selling off the businesses they operate. Still, certain industries remain in government hands. Military operations are always government-controlled; often, so are such municipal services as power generation, port operations, infrastructure development, and strategic industries like natural resources such as oil or other minerals. What is "strategic" depends on what the country produces. In any event, governments certainly need everything from stationery to cars, so even if a government does not operate major industries, it is a consumer of goods and services.

Government sales sometimes require you to use a local agent, but sometimes you can sell directly. There is no rule of thumb; you must ask. Even if you can sell directly, you may wish to use an agent to provide the local contact that helps the sale and offers after-sale support.

All governments will have contracting methods. How you contract with the government often will be based on the size of the order. The larger the order, the more complex the winning process becomes and so too the method of selling or entry strategy. Sales to governments are achieved by direct invitations to bid, direct contracts or tender offers. Generally, the latter requires a local agent to watch the announcements and get the tender documents to you.

Once you win an order, you will want to try to get the government to waive its sovereign immunity. This concept means that a government is immune from a lawsuit on its activities related to being a government. If the government is successful in such a claim, and it has not paid you, you will be out of luck. This can be a touchy area, so use good counsel in this regard. In addition, governments have unique rules for payments, paperwork and the like—different for each country.

MARKET-ENTRY STRATEGIES (continued)

FOREIGN OPERATIONS

Until now, we have been reviewing market-entry strategies that you accomplish from home. Now we will examine efforts that involve your company setting up operations in a foreign country. A major difference between the strategies is how much of the local operation do you own. If it is 100 percent owned by your company, it is a **foreign operation.** Its purpose can be to market, manufacture, offer after-sale services, do worldwide financial accounting or any other functional aspect of running your company.

If any other company or person owns any part of the operation, or if the foreign activity is conducted by anyone other than your company's staff, the effort becomes one called a **joint venture** or **strategic alliance.**

A **local operation** solely owned by your company is for any purpose to achieve the business needs. It may accomplish all of the activities of a business or any one or more of the subsets of activities a business requires.

All foreign operations have certain elements in common:

- A large capital commitment

- A commitment of time and longevity in the market

- Your being subject to all local laws and conditions

- Requirement for a business plan

- Requirement for a good reason to be there (Good reason: to produce at a lower price, to be closer to your markets)

- Mastery of the mating dance

(JOINT VENTURES AND STRATEGIC ALLIANCES)

Joint Venture

This is a separate business organization resulting from the contributions of two or more companies and owned by them as well. Its goal is to be a separate business, rather than to perform one or more subsets of activities a business requires.

Strategic Alliance

This is a cooperative relationship whereby two or more companies share or combine resources to accomplish a result. The combined effort may not be a separate business, but rather a subset of activity. For example, large pharmaceutical companies have often used smaller research and development companies to develop new drugs, which the larger company later markets for the financial benefits of both. The two companies remain separate.

Select the market-entry strategy suitable for your company and your target country. _____

List the decisions and steps you need to make to implement this choice.

1. _____

2. _____

3. _____

4. _____

5. _____

CUSTOMIZE TO THE CULTURE

If you visit McDonald's in Moscow, Singapore, Cairo or Mexico City, you will know with absolute certainty that you are in a McDonald's. You will recognize the colors, the menus and probably be able to order without even asking if Big Macs are on the menu. There will be differences, however, because each location has been customized to the culture. You won't get pork sausages in Muslim countries, and McDonald's in Southeast Asia serves iced tea rather than orange soda. These differences are a result of attention to the details of culture.

Laundry detergent sells better in Poland when the labels are badly translated into Polish. Foreigners who haven't yet learned the nuances of the language are somehow more trustworthy to the public. Stores and offices in parts of Asia must be placed in harmony with the principles of *feng shui* or the local staff believe the results will be disaster. Images of the cowboy don't sell Marlboro cigarettes in Chile; for Americans this folklore character is a hero, but for Chileans it's only a job.

Color and symbol can be of major importance too. The color of mourning in the West is black, but it is white in Asia, purple in Brazil and yellow in Mexico. Green is a fortunate color in Islam, but it means death in parts of Asia and is considered the color of earth and money in the West. If your product or its package is the wrong color, you will lose sales.

Learning the differences resulting from culture can spell the difference between success and failure in a market, especially for consumer products. The points to remember for culture are few, but their impact can be major.

It is important to review culture and its impacts on your international business. Earlier we looked at culture as it affects whether you have a market. Since what you sell determines whether you have a market and what you sell is ultimately affected by culture, adjustments may be in order. Two other areas may need adjustment for culture—management methods and business practices.

KNOW YOUR CUSTOMER

Knowing your customer is as important abroad as it is at home. When you understand the fundamental patterns of culture and how they are interrelated, you will be more effective in interacting with foreign clients and colleagues and in making sales. Culture is a strong influence; all peoples believe their culture to be superior, because people are ethnocentrist.

We recall that culture is the sum of total beliefs, rules, techniques, institutions and artifacts that characterize a group of people. Culture allows people to define their belonging to a group, what is acceptable behavior and what is not. It is learned and shared by the group. So if you want to make sales to the group, it is axiomatic that you won't if you offend their sensibilities. It took Nestle two years in the late eighties to combat rumors that some of their products sold in Muslim countries contained pork and were not halal, the equivalent of kosher.

The word "cultural" is interchangeable with "sociocultural." Fortunately, there are many ways to learn the culture of another country. You can study anthropology, literature, various business books that review the culture of countries, or even travel and experience the culture of another place. And, of course, you can hire a consultant.

Some aspects of culture are the same from one country to another. Religion is one of these characteristics. People who are Orthodox follow a different calendar and celebrate Easter at a different time of year than Roman Catholics. Thus a Russian, Greek or Finnish Orthodox would not be working the same day on which Good Friday fell. Another fact is that people retain much of their cultural heritage even if they leave their country of origin. So if you meet a Brazilian living in Shanghai, look at Brazilian culture to understand this person. Even later generations of Brazilians living in China will retain their family characteristics.

The areas to run a culture check on your behavior and product presentation fall into certain categories.

KNOW YOUR CUSTOMER (continued)

Business Practices and Social Etiquette

► Greetings

► How to address people

► Conversation

► Eye contact, body posture and spatial distance

► Sensitivities

► Table manners

► Gender—How does the culture treat women in business?

► Business negotiating style

► Time of appointments

► How much to put into the contract

► Attitude toward money and work

For example, Americans believe that "time is money." Therefore, meetings should begin punctually and get to the points of importance quickly. These are price, quality and quantity. Americans also want clear and detailed contracts, perhaps more so than any other group. Americans are less interested in relationship, trust and sincerity—qualities developed over time and essential in many cultures for successful business. Americans are less ceremonial about business meetings, but do expect a strong handshake, a smile and eye contact. These acts convey confidence and trustworthiness. Americans use many metaphors relating to sports, so this is a good conversational tactic to gain confidence.

Management Methods

► Office organization

► Organizational style and culture

► Management style

For example, a production manager had been sent to Peru from the United States, where he instituted a democratic decision-making style. Shortly afterwards, local employees began quitting. Latins were used to the authoritarian style of the patron. The locals considered anything less to be incompetent.

COMPONENTS OF CULTURE

Most agree that there are nine major components of culture. They are aesthetics, attitudes and beliefs, religion, material culture, education, language, societal organizations, legal characteristics and political structures. If you refer back to Part 2 now, you will see a much longer list, which was designed to provide more detail. Each of those details will fit into one of these major categories.

For your use, however, here are some more examples. As you read each one, think of your own country, ethnic group and family to identify your own cultural beliefs. At the end of each section make some notes on them.

Aesthetics

This is a group's sense of good taste, beauty and a way to express a communal soul. It is demonstrated by art, music, theater, symbols, folklore and dance. Numbers have many meanings. For Americans, a lucky number is 7. For Chinese, 8 is the lucky number. Avoid 4, however; it has the same sound in Chinese as the word death.

Attitudes and Beliefs

Attitudes influence nearly every aspect of life and bring a sense of order to a group. For business people, certain attitudes toward time, achievement, work and change are important to keep in mind. Middle Eastern and some Asian and Latin American cultures place a lesser emphasis on time and promptness than Americans or Europeans. Those of us who are Western must learn to be patient if we are to succeed in cultures where time has less value. Have a long look at this attitude and the others important to business dealings when looking at a target market.

MORE CULTURAL COMPONENTS AHEAD...

Religion

Religion is an enormously influential cultural component on which an entire book could be written. Religion can influence what holidays are celebrated, dietary patterns, the role of women as workers, the hours and days of work and attitudes toward work. For example, Protestants, Shintos and Confucians believe that one's duty is to glorify God by hard work. In some countries, particularly Southeast Asia, where several religious groups coexist, there are many weeks when several different religious holidays are celebrated by everyone. An example is the period of Chinese New Year and the end of Ramadan. The largest groups are Christians, Muslims, Hindus and Buddhists.

Material Culture

All man-made objects and the method of their manufacture is material culture. Also included are why objects are made and who makes them. Material culture affects what products are available and what production methods are employed, locally. A farmer who is used to fixing his equipment will find the Western throw-away mentality difficult to incorporate into his life. If your product is a "disposable," the farmer may not be a customer. In Botswana, a four-man brick press will produce only 1,500 bricks a day, and technology of use for the operators will be manageable. The production method will be compatible with their material culture.

Education

How well a society is educated is a major indicator of its economic strength and its ability to provide a literate and skilled workforce. The higher the education level of a society, generally the greater the mass purchasing power of the members. Such a society will also have more working women and therefore later marriages, a lower birth rate, and less free time. A marketing program must take into account the education factor.

COMPONENTS OF CULTURE (continued)

Language

Language includes unspoken body language, facial expressions and body position. It is often one of the factors that defines national cohesion. A country with more than one language can also suffer the potential of division; Canada, for example, argues over French and English. For business of course, the issue is to communicate to the customer. Use a translator for conversation if you are not fluent in the local language. For product literature and advertising, a double translation is urged to avoid language errors. This means having the material translated from your language to theirs and back again, using a translator with native skills in each language.

Examples of language errors are very funny in hindsight, but awful in practice. Kentucky Fried Chicken's slogan, "Finger Lickin' Good," in Mandarin became, "So good you suck your fingers." The Jolly Green Giant in Arabic was the "intimidating green ogre." "Let Hertz put you in the driver's seat," in Spanish became, "Let Hertz make you a chauffeur." No more need be said on this point.

Societal Organizations

Every society has structures or organizations. Two classes of institutions include groups based on kinship or family and those created by choice or free association. You can use these organizations to target your customer and to understand the culture. Names and their order of use is a reflection of kinship. Latins and Koreans have the given name, the paternal name and last the maternal name. An initial meeting will often include a discussion of the family tree. This is so even in cultures where both family names are not used. Family lineage and those other groups to which you choose to belong are methods by which to judge you and to know you.

How Does Culture Affect My Product or Service?

What are the elements of culture important to your product or service in the target country? _____

_____

_____

_____

_____

What changes in the product or service do you anticipate? _____

_____

_____

_____

_____

What adaptations need to be made for your business practices and management style? _____

_____

_____

_____

_____

COMPONENTS OF CULTURE (continued)

How to Reduce Culture Shock

► Realize cultures might be different from your own.

► Read and learn about the culture.

► Find a cultural mentor.

► Withhold judgment about the new culture and its people.

► Recognize that the negative feelings you may have are appropriate for this phase of adjustment (i.e., letdowns, annoyances and irritations are to be expected).

► Keep a sense of humor about yourself and your situation.

► Learn what is working well and what is not. Why is this the case?

► Be flexible with yourself and those in the host country.

► Adapt your business and social behavior and product to the culture of the target market.

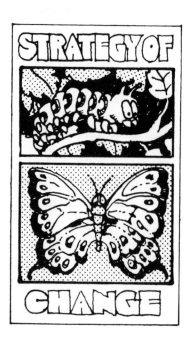

P A R T

4

International Business Basics

LEARN THE LANGUAGE OF FOREIGN TRADE

A topic that need not have customized training is the language of international business. This subject falls into two areas: foreign languages and the terms used in foreign trade.

Worldwide, the language of business is English and many people speak it well enough to do business. Rest assured it is not necessary to speak in a foreign language to do business. Knowing the local language will enable you to interact more easily. If you are selling consumer products, you need to adapt your product presentation to the local language and all its nuances. It is always better to be able to converse in the local language if you will be spending any amount of time in a country. If you speak the local language, it is a compliment, but not a prerequisite.

Of course, if you and those with whom you must deal cannot speak the same language, you will need a translator to help you communicate. At the early stages of foreign trade, a company should only work with others that do speak the same language. Once you start using translators, the risks of errors in transmission rise, and some of them are not readily caught by the novice.

Translators in foreign countries can be found through your local embassy, your hotel concierge, the yellow pages and through business center offices that offer temporary services to traveling business people. I have often used my taxi driver! Just ask the drivers in front of the hotel to find one who speaks your language.

Learning a foreign language is time consuming, but worthwhile. Many programs are available to suit your budget, timetable and preferred method of learning.

What is the language of your target? How prevalent is the use of your native language? Do you need a translator?

TERMS OF TRADE AND BUSINESS

There are new terms to use and understand in foreign trade, and even some old terms that have a new meaning. When you study the various subjects of trade, each will have a vocabulary where you will find new terms and meanings. Take a moment to consider the meaning of trade terms. Old words with new meanings must be watched closely because your familiarity with old words may cause you to overlook the consequences of the new meaning. As a precaution, when dealing with others, confirm your mutual understanding of trade terms. You will be surprised at the differences in meaning and understanding.

Shipping terms is one major area where confirmation of terms' meanings is necessary for everyone worldwide, even for very experienced business people. More familiar terms include:

- Free on Board (FOB)

- Cost Insurance Freight (CIF)

- Cost and Freight Only, no insurance (CFR)

These acronyms are shipping terms that govern only the act of delivery in any commercial transaction, domestic or international. Shipping terms are a shorthand to reflect the parties' decision of who arranges shipping and insurance, and who bears the risk of loss, i.e., when does the risk shift.

Every country has shipping terms, but like many other aspects of trade, domestic and international, we suffer from having different meanings for the same words or acronyms. For example, the Uniform Commercial Code (UCC), is U.S. law of trade and other matters like secured transactions for goods. INternational COmmercial TERMS (INCOTERMS) are international and have been designed to create uniformity. The International Chamber of Commerce (ICC), which publishes INCOTERMS as a reference standard for shipping terms used internationally, can be contacted in New York or Paris for a copy. While it is not law, INCOTERMS are usages of trade and therefore have great force, as if they were law. As of January 1, 1994, INCOTERMS are required if you are using international letters of credit and documents for examination and payment.

A Word of Caution

Some words have different meanings. If you are from the United States, you know the UCC meaning. If you are from Britain, these words have a meaning from the Law of Sales and now the EC definition. If you have been trading internationally for a while, you may know the INCOTERMS definition. The meanings are different. For example, the term CIF under INCOTERMS means that the seller arranges the shipping and insurance and transfers risk of loss of the goods when they are placed in possession of the carrier. When the seller is entitled to get paid has nothing to do with the shipping term selected. This issue is decided in the other terms of the agreement. This is not necessarily what is understood in other definitions of CIF. Unless you and the buyer attach the same meaning and consequences to the words, something is bound not to happen right.

Even experienced international businesspeople know that caution with words and their meaning is necessary. Make it a practice to verify your understanding of words used in all your communications, whether spoken or written and do so without embarrassment. Everyone will be more at ease if what you write and say is clear. Lastly, avoid colloquialisms, jargon, slang and polysyllabic words. Keep it simple and straightforward and your conversations will flow.

EXPAND YOUR INTERNATIONAL TRADE VOCABULARY

Producing a complete glossary of all international trade terms would be impossible. A good up-to-date dictionary will offer you definitions when you are in need. In the meantime, here are a few terms you may find useful.

AIRWAY BILL. A document showing that an air carrier has possession of the goods. It is a bill of lading for air transport.

ATA CARNET. A document permitting you to carry samples into a country without paying duty.

BILL OF LADING. A contract between the owner of goods and the carrier. It evidences that the carrier has possession of the goods.

CERTIFICATE OF ORIGIN. A document that shows where goods are from and is usually produced by a chamber of commerce.

CUSTOMS. The government department responsible for collecting import duties and enforcing export control and border laws.

DOCUMENTATION. All the papers necessary for a shipment to leave one country and enter another. You can prepare this paperwork yourself or hire a freight forwarder to do it. Documentation includes a commercial invoice, bill of lading, consular invoice, certificate of origin, inspection certificate, dock or warehouse receipt, insurance certificate, export license, and export packing list. Some or all of these may be required by law or by your contract.

DOCUMENTARY LETTER OF CREDIT. A letter of credit for which the issuing bank requires papers that prove the goods are shipped and that title has passed to the buyer before it will release payment.

EX-SHIP. A shipping term that means the seller makes the goods available to the buyer on board the ship at the destination named in the contract.

EX-WORKS. Another shipping term that means the seller makes the goods available at the factory door.

FREE TRADE ZONE (FTZ). A place set aside by a government in which special rules apply as duties and customs rules. Often local assembly and re-export are encouraged in FTZs, as are repackaging and bonded warehouse services. Many FTZs exist around the world.

FOREIGN CREDIT INSURANCE. Insurance from your government that you get paid for your international sales.

GATT. The General Agreement on Tariffs and Trade, a multilateral treaty signed by more than 80 countries. It provides a set of rules for trade policy and a means for settling disputes among member countries.

HARMONIZED SYSTEM (HS). A method of classifying products to simplify exporting codes internationally. A man's leather shoe would have the same code number in many countries so you could look up the duties and quotas under the number.

NIC. A newly industrialized country, one that has enjoyed rapid economic growth and can be described as middle income.

NONTARIFF BARRIER. Market-entry impediments such as product requirements, restrictions, quotas, labeling and packaging rules and local agent requirements.

PRO FORMA INVOICE. A quotation.

SITC. Standard Industrial Trade Classification developed by the United Nations as an international classification system. It is nearly identical to the HS.

TRADEMARK. Some words or images associated with a product, such as the clown image of Ronald McDonald.

REDO YOUR BUSINESS PLAN

Many of you have at some time or another written a business plan. The vogue of the 1980s was the entrepreneur and venture capital, so most business people have heard the words "business plan." Those who had one felt smug that they were in the crowd. Those who did not shuddered in fear that failure loomed around the corner if one did not have one. Indeed, statistics show that most business fail because of mismanagement. And business planning is the essence of management.

Here is your chance to create another or the first. If this plan is your first, then you should get a book or other aid to writing a business plan and use this chapter for the international component. Those of you with a plan will be amending several parts to add international components.

Before reviewing the international changes, let's look generally at various reasons for writing business plans. Some major ones are:

- A business plan is a *development tool,* a road map for success. The plan becomes a detailed to-do list, setting realistic goals and delegating assignments. It keeps you on track in all stages of your business.

- A plan is a *management and planning guide.* As such, the plan becomes the operating bible or the strategic plan of the business. You can't predict the future; the best you can do is monitor, measure actual vs. predicted results, and take corrective action. Strategic planning forces you to identify goals, strategies and objectives in a realistic manner.

- A phrase in vogue in the 1990s is a *"mission statement,"* which a plan is as well.

- And last, a plan is a financing tool. The business plan becomes a sales document. Sometimes plans are also used to attract key employees, large contracts and arranging strategic alliances.

For your international expansion, your plan will be mostly a development tool and a planning guide. Issues relating to the international expansion of your business will arise for the sections relating to the description of the business, the market, the competition, location, management, personnel and financial projections. In other words, most aspects of your business in some way will be affected by the decision to expand internationally.

Here is a typical table of contents for a business plan. Reflect for a moment on the subjects you may wish to consider in editing your existing plan. I've added some questions to start you thinking.

BUSINESS PLAN TABLE OF CONTENTS

I. THE BUSINESS
   A. Description of Business—What am I selling?
   B. The Market—Who is my customer? Where in the world are my markets?
   C. Competition—Who else is selling there? What are they selling and at what price?
   D. Location of Business—Do I want an office/plant elsewhere?
   E. Management—Who will do what?
   F. Personnel—Do I use agents, distributors, joint venture partners?
   G. Application and Expected Effect of Loan, New Capital or Equity— What kind of budget and financial resources will success need?
   H. Summary

II. FINANCIAL DATA
   A. Sources and Applications of Funding—Where will I get the money from and what will I use it for?
   B. Capital Equipment List—Will I need any new equipment?
   C. Balance Sheet
   D. Pro Forma Income and Cash-flow Statement
   E. Historical Financial Reports—Tell me whether my cost of goods sold is increasing. Can I reduce costs by buying or producing elsewhere or by increasing volume?
   F. Summary

III. SUPPORTING DOCUMENTS
   A. Functional Resumes
   B. References to Market Information

STRATEGIC PLANNING CHECKLIST

When you reflect on the reasons you write a business plan, you will conclude that doing the work to create a plan is strategic planning. You have been engaging in such planning while reading this book and even before you bought it. Let's look at the steps of strategic planning and consider which ones you may have already done.

☐ **Analyze a Company's External Environment.**

Have you observed foreign competition in your home turf? Or have you felt the recession of the 1990s? Are foreign markets intriguing to you because the nightly news brings them to your living room? How will you continue to collect information about your competition and your foreign markets?

☐ **Analyze the Internal Environment of the Company.**

What is the financial condition of the company? Are profit margins decreasing? Do you forecast reduced profits because of an increasing cost of goods sold? Can you make changes to address the problem? Will it be enough? Do you have the personnel and know-how to change how you do business to address the international markets that are available to you?

☐ **Define the Mission of the Company.**

Increasing sales through foreign market development is a mission. Making the best widget in the world is too, as is being the market leader or having a significant share.

☐ **Set Corporate Objectives.**

What are the goals? A goal can be to develop the ability of the business to be competitive in foreign markets. This defines the firm's course within the mission.

☐ **Quantify Goals.**

These need not be numerical. A goal can be to develop a seven- to ten-year plan to develop all foreign markets of the company.

□ **Formulate Strategy.**

What is your action plan? Defining the four Ps is part of the strategy. The business plan is the written document that embodies the strategy. It answers
- What you sell
- How you will sell it
- What must be done to sell it
- Who will sell it
- How much will be spent to do it

□ **Make Tactical Plans.**

What is your plan of operation in detail with a timetable?
- Sales forecasts
- Budgets
- Pricing policies
- Product characteristics
- Promotional plans
- Details of arrangements with foreign representatives
- Costs of developing foreign markets

The bottom line is that you are translating a global business strategy into a series of actions.

Check which steps you have already done. Now list the strategic steps you still need to take.

_____

_____

_____

ASSEMBLE YOUR PROFESSIONAL BACK-UP TEAM

Every new or existing business, whether or not you trade internationally, has functional needs in accounting, law, banking, and insurance. Some have these functions managed by in-house staff; in others, independent businesses provide these services. For the sake of easier understanding we will call these people "professionals," though technically not all are. Either way, these professionals will have to upgrade their knowledge to be able to represent you properly. Or, you may find you need another set of professionals to handle your international needs. Do not be surprised if your existing professionals lack the knowledge or experience to guide you. For service providers too, the world is new.

Your in-house staff members need to develop their skills and to be given the time to do so. Both in-house and outside professionals will catch on, or else move out. There are people with the skills you need and you do not have time to wait.

But this book is not about them; it is about and for you. It is designed to equip you to develop, negotiate and close new businesses in foreign countries. You, too, must learn new skills in the same four areas as your professional service providers in order to accomplish this goal. The information you will gather about these areas will be incorporated into your business plan and, of course, into the marketing plan. To some extent it will affect the priority of steps you take or the events that occur. To avoid being out of sync, check out the information first.

Take the Pulse

Who are your service providers and what is their experience and skill in the international arena? Call each one and discuss your plans and ask what are their strengths and weaknesses. Also, find out how they are addressing their knowledge gaps.

SERVICE & NAME OF FIRM	SKILLS AND EXPERIENCE
• Accounting	
• Attorneys	
• Banking	
• Insurance	

How are these four areas going to fit into your foreign market efforts? What do you need to look at while planning your foreign market strategy?

ACCOUNTING AND FINANCIAL MANAGEMENT

Accounting and financial management serve several important functions: recording results, complying with tax responsibilities and forecasting for planning purposes. All three are essential for management to make the right decisions. This is no less true for international trade.

The occasions management consults with the accounting department in order to observe results, pay taxes and plan are further itemized on the next pages. Take a minute now and check off each activity you now engage in. Every one of these accounting- and financial-management activities will occur for your international business. As you undergo the planning process, keep them in mind and obtain the information you need. Until you are well versed in foreign trade, you will come across some twists and turns of which you know nothing now. Your existing accounting and financial management systems will not record, or alert you when you hit some of these new areas.

Case Study: Does 1 Franc = 1 Naira = 1 Yen?

Consider a company that sells the same product in more than 30 foreign markets. A preliminary decision was made to price and collect payment only in French francs. When the chief executive officer (CEO) was asked if the comptroller had had a chance to review the pricing and collection strategy, he said no. It seemed that the comptroller did not understand the relative value of foreign currencies; he could not forecast the cash flow from around the world or assist the CEO to develop a method to collect the revenue from worldwide distributors. The CEO was forced to make decisions on important matters, such as pricing and a banking system for collecting the revenues, by himself. Moreover, no system was being developed to collect information from the customers and the market about pricing relative to currency differentials to assist the CEO in the future adjustments of the business direction.

What would you suggest to the CEO and comptroller?

_____

_____

_____

Accounting and Financial Management Activities

Which ones do you do? Some may be beyond your present needs at this stage in the development of your business. But knowing about them now will help you identify the next development phase of your business and prepare for the twists and turns in the road.

Financial Statements

Sourcing Debt and/or Equity Internationally

Capital Budgeting

Direct Foreign Investment

Long-term Financing Decisions

Multinational Capital Budgeting

Financial Planning Managing

Import/Export Financing

Foreign Exchange Exposure

Working Capital Management

Managing Transaction Exposure

Performance Evaluation and Controls

International Banking

Others

Handling Foreign Taxes

Pause for a moment to consider which taxes also fit into your banking needs, your marketing planning and any other management decisions you will make.

Some taxes to consider are:

- Value added taxes

- Foreign income taxes

- Foreign withholding taxes

LAW

The following information will help you create for your business a standard agreement. This is one of the most important things you can do in foreign business. You must devote energy and time to this task before trade occurs; the angst and damage that can result from not doing it far outweigh the effort required to do it right. First, work out the business decisions and policies you want to protect in your agreements and documentation with your lawyer *before* you begin to negotiate the deal!

The suggestions and principles identified in this section result from a comparison of the laws of the various legal systems around the world, including the body of law known as international law. After you understand the points, you should create an operating procedure with standard documents.

There are three major new subjects to understand:

1. What law, trade or industry practice governs your international business?

2. Do you have a contract?

3. What happens if something goes wrong?

What Law, Industry or Trade Practice Governs You?

International law governs international trade. Local law governs anything that happens inside a country. Therefore, you need to know both. We reviewed local law requirements when we discussed market ingredients.

International law is generally the law found in treaties or conventions, also known as **agreements between nations.** Many treaties exist that govern international trade and other relevant areas such as dispute resolution. There is also a body of law that is called **conflicts of law** and another called **choice of law.** These guide a judge or arbitrator in selecting the law that should be applied to a situation. Ultimately, the judge must select the law of one party's country or another. This area of law is not precise, so there is uncertainty until you know what the judge does.

The Four Rules of International Trade

RULE #1: *You and your trade partner make the rules.*

All laws, to a large extent, are designed to supply a rule to govern or resolve relationships where you do not select the way you want the matter resolved. In commercial dealings, this is especially true.

The more you clarify with your trading partner in your documents, the less is left to chance. Unless you are engaging in actions that are criminal or illegal (and you know what is criminal or illegal generally), everything else you do or agree upon is okay.

RULE #2: *If you do not make the rules, someone else, the judge or arbitrator, will.*

Legal systems are like the default drives on your computer: If you do not tell the computer where to go, it has an internal system that makes the choice for you. Likewise, you will be stuck with a rule that resolves your situation in a way that may be unacceptable to you because the judge or arbitrator will have to select rules to resolve your dispute.

This is why it is so important to detail from start to finish what will happen, who does what, when, where and how. What do you want to happen if something goes wrong? How do you want to be compensated if you are damaged? Walk through the transaction mentally to look at the steps. Write it all down. These are the rules. Make the picture clear.

RULES 3 AND 4 AHEAD...

LAW (continued)

Fortunately, there is plenty of shorthand available, so your contracts and documents do not have to weigh a ton. All you need to do is learn the shorthand. The following is only an introduction to the shorthand:

- Seller's name, address, phone, fax, contact person

- Buyer's name, address, phone, fax, contact person

- What is being sold

- The quantity

- The price

- A description or quality of the items sold

- Where it will be delivered

- Shipping terms—how will it be shipped?

- How will you be paid

- Who will get the insurance

- Any additional needs—be practical; do not think legal

> ## RULE #3: All contracts must state the basic four.

- ✓ **PRODUCT**
- ✓ **PRICE**
- ✓ **QUANTITY**
- ✓ **DESCRIPTION**

If you boil all the rules of law from legal systems around the world, some basic principles emerge. For commercial transactions, you have much uniformity around the world. Fortunately, basic contract law remains based on the agreement of the parties. Business people still decide what to sell, at what price and what quantity and quality. No legal system will change this commercial reality. Thus, we have the *"basic four."*

> ## RULE #4: Contracts need nothing else except the basic four to be a contract.

Do We Have a Deal? What Are My Obligations?

Many rules of law in all countries have been developed to determine whether people have a contract. A first common rule is whether the parties have agreed upon the basic terms—the basic four. Of course, contracts for the sale of goods include many more terms, such as specifications, place and time of delivery, extent of liability, method of dispute settlement, method of payment, shipping responsibility, trade standards, default, insurance and many others. These result from your business policy and negotiations. While these other terms can be extremely important, their absence from an agreement does not affect the question of whether there is a contract. You could and should include many possible subjects in your standard contract. Of course, your product and company policy will determine which ones are important.

Your obligations are to buy or sell consistently with the basic four and to fulfill every other term you and your trading partner put into the agreement.

Sales agreements are as varied as the goods sold. A sales contract for automobile parts necessarily differs from a contract to buy wheat. But while the details vary considerably, common subjects appear in most sales agreements.

LAW (continued)

Generally, if the four material terms are accepted, there is a contract. How this works in day-to-day business is helpful to review and will illustrate the point.

- **EXAMPLE ONE:** Seller offers potential buyer one hundred tons of Grade A cement at $3.00 per ton. He does this in writing and sends the offer by FAX. Buyer answers, "Yes, this is OK." There is a deal.

- **EXAMPLE TWO:** Same offer. Buyer answers, "Yes, but I want to pay $2.95 per ton." No deal until seller replies "OK at $2.95."

- **EXAMPLE THREE:** Same offer. Buyer answers "Yes, but I want the cement delivered by March 27, 19XX." There is a deal under both U.S. law and international law, as found in the UN Convention on Contracts for the International Sale of Goods (CISG), unless the change, or new term materially alters the original offer.

Thus, unless the acceptance mirrors exactly the original offer, you run the risk of disagreement on whether you have a deal. This is because parties can argue over what is material. A simple solution is to insert a sentence or two along these lines, "This offer is expressly limited to its terms and can only be accepted in full. No additional or different terms are acceptable to be included in any reply." This type of clarification is useful especially where you do not have face-to-face negotiations or a working relationship with a trading partner.

You can negotiate how all obligations are resolved. You should be able to do so during the negotiating stage *and* before you ask your lawyer to draft a contract. If you do not exercise your right to determine the answers to these questions, you waive an important opportunity. It is almost as bad as letting another person set your price. You can select the legal results applicable to your contracts if you become assertive and learn your rights. The benefits of clarity to both sides will be profound.

Does It Have to Be in Writing?

The answer to the question of whether an agreement must be in writing illustrates a difference between the law of many countries, the treaty called the U.N. Convention on Contracts for the International Sale of Goods (CISG), or international law of many countries. The laws of many countries require "some writing" for a contract over $500 to be enforceable; the CISG does not. Keep in mind that certain terms such as waivers or other terms must be in writing. Though you may have a contract, you will not have an agreement over any points that must be in writing. Examples of two very important subjects include first, an election to arbitrate disputes rather than litigate; and second, waivers of product liability. No formal document is necessary, just some written memo of the material terms. Again, these are price, quantity, quality, and subject. To resolve this difference your quotes and standard agreement can state, "ABC Company requires all agreements to be in writing."

The FAX Can Be Your Contract

The good news is that a FAX can be the writing in most countries and most circumstances! But certain government contracting cannot be by FAX. As a general rule, FAX is fine for commercial transactions. To be absolutely certain, you can add another sentence to your quote and agreement, "We agree to be bound by FAX."

The last point to make is that original signatures are not necessary unless you so require them. Any mark indicating your assent can be enough.

In conclusion, if your FAX contains the basic four and a mark indicating assent, you have a legally enforceable deal. Practically speaking, you should include several other terms to resolve other practical issues. In the end, once you develop your company policy on what else should be included, you are on your way to using your FAX to sell worldwide.

LAW (continued)

What Happens if Something Goes Wrong?

Here is another area where some advance planning can offer more certainty of result and orchestrate the manner in which disputes are resolved, thus reducing the cost and time involved. Three questions arise in this area.

1. What law will apply? This answers such questions as who is wrong, what do you get if there is a breach.

2. How do you resolve your disputes?

3. Where do you go to do so?

Each question can be handled by contract and is a part of your standard negotiation for an international transaction. Discuss it all with your business partner *while* negotiating, not after.

The first question, what law will apply, is generally the hardest. You will want the law of your country, and the other party will want his or hers. The CISG is a solution for transactions involving the sale of goods. Services, however, do not fall under the convention, so for such contracts you will have to deal with this question. You will have to learn something about the laws of the other country to decide which law to apply. You can design your own solutions to specific questions that may arise. For example, you can adopt a measure of damages that you both find fair. Or you can define what is a breach. These contractual provisions will govern over and above any legal system that is applied.

Dispute resolution, the second question, is generally easy to resolve, since everyone has had a bad experience. Three methods of rational dispute resolution are possible: litigation or court, arbitration and mediation or reconciliation. Each method has differing costs, time tables and demands in terms of who must be involved. All of them permit the parties to adopt a legal system to apply and all will choose one to follow if you do not.

Generally, litigation is the most expensive and time consuming and requires lawyers. It is highly rigid and ritualistic in its rules of procedure. It is only done in courts by judges from the country where the trial is being held. Therefore, litigation has the highest possibility for local bias. Americans and Westerners tend to be comfortable with litigation.

Arbitration is far less rigid, time consuming and does not *require* lawyers. Nevertheless, arbitrating any significant matter without a lawyer is a bad idea. Another great difference between litigation and arbitration is that organizations that offer arbitration are often international in nature and, therefore, there is less potential for bias. Arbitration organizations also have offices in many countries, so you get a geographic advantage that is lost with litigation. Arbitration systems can offer arbitrators with certain industry expertise, which can often be very helpful. The procedure is far less formal and quicker. Europeans have a cultural preference for arbitration.

Mediation and reconciliation seek to achieve a mutually agreeable solution to a problem rather than render a decision, as in an arbitration or litigation. This is more comfortable for Asians than for Westerners.

The method of dispute resolution upon which you agree must be in writing, especially if you choose to give up your right to litigate. In addition to electing a non-court method to use, you will also need to select the organization to run the procedure and the city in which to do so.

A litigation is generally restricted to a court, all of which have limited jurisdiction or authority over what type of cases they may hear. Ask your lawyer which court can hear your case. An arbitration and mediation can be heard by any number of organizations that offer these services for which you pay. Or you can conduct your own private session by agreeing in your contract on a third party who will be your arbitrator or mediator.

Where you resolve a dispute is simply a matter of where the organization you have selected has offices and a place that is mutually convenient and agreeable for both parties. Often when both parties have to travel the same distance to resolve disputes, no one travels at all.

Is your law firm knowledgeable in international trade? List what will be included in your standard contracts.

_____

_____

_____

BANKING

What will you need from your banker? In addition to what you now get, you will need:

- A way to get paid from foreigners

- A bank in a foreign country to use for local needs or for special needs of a transaction

- Information about the market and a credit report on your customer

- Credit and loans

- Assistance in obtaining payment insurance

Some banks only conduct domestic business. You need to inquire what international services your bank offers and if it has none, locate a bank that does. Take time to learn about worldwide banking services and incorporate them into your planning.

International banks facilitate and support firms doing international business in the following ways:

- Financing imports and exports

- Trading foreign exchange and currency options

- Borrowing and lending in international currency markets

- Organizing or participating in international loan syndications

- Underwriting both Eurobonds and foreign bonds

- Providing international cash management

- Soliciting local currency deposits and loans with an intent to operate as a full-service local bank

- Supplying information and advice to clients

Which services does your bank offer? _____

_____

What are your needs? _____

_____

All of these services are important, but we will only focus on methods of getting paid. International transactions can be paid by the following methods. Each has a different level of risk of nonpayment.

▶ *Cash in advance or cash on delivery (C.O.D.):* With this method, you receive payment before shipping.

▶ *Letter of credit (L/C):* An L/C is really a letter from the importer to its bank telling the bank to pay the seller when the paperwork is presented that shows that the goods have been shipped. It places a third party in possession of the money. There are many kinds of letters of credit to solve several issues that arise. These include: irrevocable letter, confirmed, divisible, etc.

▶ *Bills of exchange:* This is the opposite of an L/C, in that the instruction is from the exporter to the buyer to pay against shipment. Like L/Cs, several types exist, including sight drafts, time drafts, trade acceptance, authority to purchase, and others.

▶ *Open account:* This method is your standard account, with terms. A foreign customer should be checked out before extending credit. In some industries business is done only with open accounts. If this is the case, you need to set a company policy on the maximum amount on which you will extend credit without either a credit check or other security.

▶ *Consignments:* You give the merchandise and wait to get paid if there are sales.

▶ *Countertrade or noncash payment methods:* Countertrade includes barter, offset, counterpurchase and buyback. Each method exchanges goods rather than money. These methods are complicated and require special know-how. In some countries and for certain kinds of transactions, this method is the only way you can do business.

▶ *Forfaiting:* This method is factoring without recourse. You sell your receivables at a discount.

Obviously, getting paid is very important and not simple. You will find each market has some different needs. First learn about the different methods.

INSURANCE

Any form of insurance available domestically is generally available in any other country. This section outlines types applicable to international trade. These are

- Insuring for injury due to your product or service to a foreign customer

- Insuring during transportation

- Insuring that you get paid

- Insuring against risks, such as political, economic or otherwise

Each of these is familiar to you and can be addressed by inquiring with your insurance carrier to extend coverage. The exception may be insuring that you get paid, so this is the only form this section will cover.

Export credits can be insured either by private or public organizations, against both commercial and political risk. Like any insurance, the cost will vary with the degree of risk perceived by the insurance underwriter.

Your domestic carrier should be able to direct you to private companies that offer credit insurance. So can your new international bank. When you speak with your own national government and the foreign one, ask this question:

What export/import credit guarantee programs do you offer? _____

_____

_____

_____

_____

_____

TRAIN AND EDUCATE YOUR STAFF

Having an international outlook, a global approach, in your business requires that everyone in your organization be involved. From the president and chairman of the board to the clerk in the mailroom—each person needs to be aware of the differences in activities that will be a part of a global approach to business. Some will have to do and learn more than others. It all starts at the top, however, with the plan being accepted and approved so that it can be implemented.

Unless top management fully accepts the choice to globalize a business by looking at foreign markets and understands the consequences and commits the resources of time, money and manpower, the game will be lost. All winning approaches begin with vision, then leadership, management and teamwork. Many companies today are learning a new game: international trade. It is much like the games we know but also has differences.

The best way to make sure that all the players know the rules and skills is to do a trial run with the target country you have been investigating. In other words, practice. The trial run is first done at home from your desk. First, management plans and mentally walks through each step of a transaction. This exercise will point out what else you need to know, where you may need expert assistance and who in your organization needs more know-how.

A SKILLS AND KNOWLEDGE INVENTORY

► Start with yourself, and make a list of the things that you already know that you need to learn.

_____

_____

_____

_____

► If you are the top in the organization, look at your subordinates. Start with the next in line and list every functional area of the business. Make notes on what you think each person will have to learn.

_____

_____

_____

_____

► Now that you have a list, the next question is how will you collect the information that you need and learn what you must know?

_____

_____

_____

_____

A Sample List

Title and Function

President, Chairman of the Board
Top management of the company
Majority shareholder
Age: 55
Started business 17 years ago
All major sales and planning

Will have to learn:

How to assess foreign markets, whether to go further, how much time to devote
How much to budget to develop each market
What tasks need to be done to develop a foreign market
To whom to delegate the tasks necessary to implement the plan
How to set realistic goals
How to measure progress

Where to get this information?

This book and others—independent research
The references listed earlier—Sources of Information on International Trade
Institutional training programs
In-house training from consulting companies

Now, for each major functional area of your company, create a list of this format.

TRAINING OPPORTUNITIES ABOUND

We are indeed fortunate today that, as part of the globalization of the world, training is available in many forms. You can have it your way too: either in-house, at a university, on an island or on your headsets while you jog. When many of you were in college, few courses were available that focused on the international aspects of any subject. Today, few subjects remain that do not have an international component. Some are entirely international in scope.

Training Program Sources Quick-Check

Training and information are available from a number of sources. The formats of these programs fall into the following categories. Place a checkmark in each box after you have requested information on available programs.

☐ Seminars or Workshops

☐ Books

☐ Conferences

☐ Audiocassettes

☐ Video/Films

☐ Formal Education Towards a Degree

☐ Continuing Education

☐ In-Company Training Programs

☐ Self-Study Texts

☐ General Periodical Literature

Almost any subject is available, presented in general terms. In-company training is often useful because it is customized to your company and product. This, of course, is not the case for any public program or literature. Many subjects need not be customized, however. Export documentation or letters of credit are examples. The planning stages or the material of this book is suitable for in-company training or consulting.

SWING INTO ACTION—
MAKE A TRIAL RUN

After a trial run from your desk, it is time to get into action in the real world. After screening for all the factors and deciding the entry strategy, you go on a trip or send someone to the target country. You could also go on a trade mission, attend a trade fair or take whatever approach you have decided on. For your first few countries, use your basic senses as the best measure of your assumptions about the market and your approach. This, of course, requires you or someone to go there on your behalf. When you return you can review your assumptions and refine your approach. No matter how thorough you are, how good your information, a firsthand look is an essential component of a successful plan.

Apart from verifying your assumptions, a firsthand look will also verify the information you have collected. Remember, no one source of information will give you everything you need to know. Equally important to remember is that information gets old quickly. The most up-to-date information is that which you gather today—from the source.

Another benefit of visiting a country is that you hone your skills in assessing it and develop the method that you will employ to present your company in foreign lands. A reality of foreign trade is that proximity is lost. Most everything will be done from a distance, so another skill will be to judge what is going on from afar. The ability to read between the lines across cultural bounds and geographic distances will become acutely necessary.

MAKE A TRIAL RUN (continued)

The Action-Plan Checklist

Before You Go:

☐ Decide who goes. You, or send a Global Guide?

☐ How? Attend a trade fair, exhibit at one or go on a trade mission?

☐ Check out the Favorite Indices when you arrive.

☐ Screen the country.

☐ Pick the market-entry strategy you think you want to use.

☐ Announce your arrival to candidates and request appointments for the first two or three days you are there.

Upon Your Return:

☐ Review, refine and adjust your plan.

☐ Decide what you learned that is specific to that market alone and what is generally applicable. For example, changing your literature will not be just for the target.

How much time will it take to see results? It should take about three months to prepare for, enter and locate the people with whom you will work in a given target country. Then another one to three months to cement the relationship. Results in the form of inquiries and orders should start in another three to twelve months. This is a conservative estimate. You may be very surprised at how fast it can work!

FAVORITE INDICES

One, some or all of the ingredients discussed in Part 2 will either close the door to a market or tell you to keep going and how. If you have gone to your target country, you are fairly certain there is a market. Once there, you will want to verify your assumptions. Here are ways to do so and collect information as well.

I always start with these steps that, admittedly, are based on pure physical observation in the country in question. They are also based on the reality of being travel weary. When you arrive in a country, you usually are hungry and tired. Maybe you need to get your hair done. So the first things to do after checking into your hotel are to shower, eat and visit the barber or hairdresser. You also will probably phone local contacts and begin making appointments.

You can tell much of what you want to know from these three factors: telephones, barber and beauty shops, and the grocery store. You also can verify your assumptions. You cannot beat the hands-on, eyes, ears, nose and touch method to identify and confirm the status of the market.

(TELEPHONES)

Take telephones. An extensive telephone system means that the government or a company invested a large amount of capital. To authorize such development, the government must have wanted the citizens of the country to talk to each other and to the rest of the world. In China, Russia and other countries, this was not the case. A lack of telephones often indicates unstable governments and, therefore, economies and cultures in which foreign investment is not welcome.

If you sold telemarketing services or wholesale long-distance telephone services, any country with few telephones would not be a market at all. The number of telephones per capita is an important statistic to understand the overall economic development of a country. For example, the United States boasts of 95 telephones per 100 households; China has 1 per 100 and Mexico only 5 per 100.

This one simple factor, telephones per household, will provide you with a wealth of information. It may or may not be critical to the sale of your product or service, but it will tell you much about the entire country.

FAVORITE INDICES (continued)

BEAUTY SALONS AND BARBERSHOPS

We all have experienced the gossip and chatter of barber and hair salons. One universal fact of life, worldwide, is this shop talk. After traveling anywhere, it feels good to get your hair done or get a shave. While there, you can overhear what the locals talk about. Talk with them. What is life like in the country? How is the future, how is it now? What are they wearing? What magazines does the shop have? Are the journals international or local? Is the newspaper free or government-censored? Do they use local or foreign shampoo and tools? Even if the locals speak a language that you do not, you will get the sense and flavor of the place.

GROCERY STORES

Have a look at what is for sale, how it is packaged and displayed; the variety; how much is imported, processed or locally produced; and how much is instant or needs to be prepared from scratch. What kind of cash registers are there? Are there freezers for food or just outdoor food stalls?

What and how people eat, as evidenced by the displays in grocery stores, reflects the quality of life of a country. If most people buy food from open food stalls without refrigeration, the people do not have electrical appliances at home either. This would indicate an underdeveloped country. The variety of food reflects the internal distribution capacity of a country. In Russia, only a few fruits and vegetables are available in winter in St. Petersburg. Therefore, we know the country lacks efficient distribution systems of roads, trains and trucks. If your product requires such a system, you'll have to bring your own trucks!

These seemingly odd ways to look at a country verify your impressions and give you the pulse of a country. They are indices of happiness, confidence in a government, freedom of expression and openness.

Now on to Conquering the Rest of the World!

After finishing the test run, you will want to survey the world and locate the markets with the highest potential and easiest access. Start with these and move toward more difficult markets. How do you survey the world and narrow the field? You continue to use the ingredients of a market to determine if a market is present for your company and to decide what are the important characteristics of a market for your company.

Next, prioritize these items. Weight the importance of the characteristic. For example, if you sell a service, such as data management for tax-revenue collection, to governments, a very important market condition is government stability. On the other hand, if you sell fast food, government stability is not so important, but a city's population is. In fact, the population per square meter is critical. When looking at markets, you will notice that some combination of factors is necessary to make this market worthwhile. Some factors may change over time, making a market one to keep your eye on or impossible to work in.

1. What factors are essential to a market for my product or service? _____

_____

2. What factors eliminate a market? _____

_____

3. What factors make a market a long-term one worth watching? _____

_____

4. When should I check this market again? _____

_____

5. List five countries where you think you may have a good market and assign the task to a staff member to collect information.

_____

_____

_____

_____

_____

GET A *GLOBAL GUIDE*

In addition to the sources of information outlined earlier, many services are available to help you begin and win at foreign trade. They range from free to costly and are varied in what types of services are offered.

You always have the option of doing everything by yourself. Keep in mind, though, that you may waste a lot of time. While you are studying a topic, your competitor is selling to your customers. You can always get more money; you can't get more time. Therefore, the primary benefit of *Global Guides* is that they save you time. Second, they save you effort and aggravation from climbing the learning curve.

Deciding what you need will be clear from the work you have done in the previous exercises. You will need information, staffing and know-how. Private and government services are outsources. Outsources can also be used as a sounding board for your plans. Once you know what you are looking for, finding it will be easy because of the proliferation of organizations offering international trade services. Your task is to match the outsource with your needs.

Why not take advantage of all there is available to help you? You never know when or where that service or bit of invaluable information will surface. Make it a habit to check all levels of information and *Global Guide* services available. This methodical approach will avoid the unpleasant situation where you learn too late something that would have changed your course.

TYPES OF *GLOBAL GUIDES*

You will notice that for both *Global Guides* and for information in the beginning of the book, the same categories exist. They are

From the public sector:

- Your government—national, state and local

- The foreign government—national, state and local

From the private sector:

- Businesses that offer services

- Trade or industry associations, including chambers of commerce

Every service, type of organization or government department is available everywhere in the world. In other words, all countries have the government and private organizations found in the following index. As with everything else in life, some are better than others. As with information, no one service will answer all your needs. A good overall plan will encompass something from each service, blending sector, services and price.

The index on the next few pages is organized by who is offering services. Each one also offers information. It is not always obvious what services each offers, so take time to ask. Each will be in the telephone or other kind of directory.

DO YOU KNOW WHERE TO FIND INFORMATION?

FINDING INFORMATION

Check first with your local and national government, then with the foreign offices, and finally with the private sector. You can start with membership or trade associations and then look at business services. This approach will cover the range of possibilities.

After reviewing the index, take out your telephone book and return to this page and make a list of the organizations you can call in your state or city to find out what they offer. Then review the list to decide which service you will look at more closely. You may already be a member or client of some.

MY GOVERNMENT

Local—City or Region

State—Provincial or Regional

National

THE (TARGET COUNTRY'S) FOREIGN GOVERNMENT

Local—City or Region

State—Provincial or Regional

National

PRIVATE SECTOR

Trade, Industry Associations or Chambers of Commerce

Business Services

INDEX OF SERVICES

Governments Offer:

National Governments (Yours and the foreign government)

—Foreign Investment Promotion Departments
—Ministries of Trade
—Ministries of Economic Development
—Industry-Specific Agencies
—Departments devoted to exporting
—Foreign trade zones
—Trade missions
—Catalog shows

State or Local Municipal Governments

—Yours and Theirs
—Departments of Economic Development
—Departments devoted to foreign trade
—Specific industry agencies
—Regional associations
—Foreign trade zones
—Trade missions
—Catalog shows

Remember that these government departments are paid for by your tax dollars. Here is a chance to get something for your money.

PRIVATE SECTOR SERVICES AHEAD...

INDEX OF SERVICES (continued)

The Private Sector

Businesses

- Transportation services:
  - —Air, Water, Land
  - —Freight Forwarders/Customs Experts
  - —Brokers/Shipping Agents & Brokers
  - —Duty Drawback Specialists
  - —Port Authorities
  - —Warehousing and Storage
  - —Packing and Crating
  - —Other Transportation-Related Services
- Telecommunications Services
- Schools and Universities
- Financial Services
  - —Banks
  - —Insurance Carriers/Agents & Brokers
  - —Foreign Currency Exchange
  - —Credit Reporting Services
  - —Consultants

- Accounting and Legal Firms
- Translation Services
- Business Services
  - —Information Resources
  - —Market Research Firms
  - —Global Marketing Advertising & Services
  - —Communication Services
  - —Executive Search Services
  - —Trade Shows and Exhibition Management
  - —Outsource *Global Guides*
  - —Technical Services (such as engineering)
  - —Products
  - —Software and Literature
  - —How-to Manuals

Membership or Trade Associations

- Specific Industry Trade Associations
- Chambers of Commerce
- International Trade Clubs
- World Trade Centers
- Exhibition Companies
- Regional Associations
- Trade Missions
- Catalog Shows

Match your needs with what is available. You will note that several organizations offer the same or similar services. Now, combine your research into an action list of who will be your *Global Guide*.

MY NEEDS	SERVICES AVAILABLE
• Information	
• Staffing	
• Know-how	

CONCLUSION

This is a time of great worldwide opportunity. As the world gets smaller and we all meet each other in trade, our chances of greater business growth increase. John F. Kennedy once said "All boats rise with the tide." So it is with increasing international trade. It is good for your company, for your country and for the rest of the world.

The world is truly your oyster. Happy harvesting.

OVER 150 BOOKS AND 35 VIDEOS AVAILABLE IN THE 50-MINUTE SERIES

We hope you enjoyed this book. If so, we have good news for you. This title is part of the best-selling *50-MINUTE*™ *Series* of books. All *Series* books are similar in size and identical in price. Many are supported with training videos.

To order *50-MINUTE* Books and Videos or request a free catalog, contact your local distributor or Crisp Publications, Inc., 1200 Hamilton Court, Menlo Park, CA 94025. Our toll-free number is (800) 442-7477.

50-Minute Series Books and Videos Subject Areas . . .

Management
Training
Human Resources
Customer Service and Sales Training
Communications
Small Business and Financial Planning
Creativity
Personal Development
Wellness
Adult Literacy and Learning
Career, Retirement and Life Planning

Other titles available from Crisp Publications in these categories

Crisp Computer Series
The Crisp Small Business & Entrepreneurship Series
Quick Read Series
Management
Personal Development
Retirement Planning